Principled Worship

Principled Worship
Biblical Guidelines for Emerging Liturgies

Sam Hamstra, Jr.

Wipf & Stock Publishers
Eugene, Oregon

PRINCIPLED WORSHIP: BIBLICAL GUIDELINES FOR EMERGING LITURGIES

Copyright © 2006 Sam Hamstra, Jr. All rights reserved. Except for brief quotations in critical publications or reviews, no part of this book may be reproduced in any manner without prior written permission from the publisher. Write: Permissions, Wipf & Stock, 199 W. 8th Ave., Suite 3, Eugene, OR 97401.

ISBN: 1-59752-523-5

Manufactured in the U.S.A.

Table of Contents

Preface — vii

Introduction — xii
    Principle #1   On the Regulative Principle for Worship

Chapter 1   Our Triune God and Worship — 1
    Principle #2   On the Initiative for Worship — 1
    Principle #3   On the Potential For Worship — 5

Chapter 2   The Person Who Worships — 11
    Principle #4   On the Heart of the Worshiper — 11
    Principle #5   On the Attitude of the Worshiper — 15
    Principle #6   On the Involvement of the Worshiper — 18
    Principle #7   On the Offerings of the Worshiper — 21

Chapter 3   The People Who Worship — 24
    Principle #8   On the Gathering for Worship — 24
    Principle #9   On the Unity of the Worshipers — 28
    Principle #10   On the Covenant of the Worshipers — 30
    Principle #11   On the Seekers Among the Worshipers — 34
    Principle #12   On the Identity of the Worshipers — 37
    Principle #13   On the Leaders of Worship — 42

Chapter 4	The Content of Worship	47
Principle #14	On the Sermon in Worship	47
Principle #15	On the Truth in Worship	50
Principle #16	On the Drama of Worship	53
Principle #17	On the Prayers of Worship	58
Principle #18	On the Gospel in Worship	61
Principle #19	On the Praise of Worship	64
Chapter 5	The Music of Worship	67
Principle #20	On the Songs of Worship	67
Principle #21	On the Sounds of Worship	72
Chapter 6	The Context for Worship	76
Principle #22	On the Culture of Worship	76
Principle #23	On the Day of Worship	81
Principle #24	On the Form and Freedom of Worship	84
Principle #25	On the Space of Worship	87
Principle #26	On the Aesthetics of Worship	91
Principle #27	On the Technology of Worship	95
Conclusion		100
Principle #28	On Daily Worship	100
Principle #29	On the Future of Worship	104
Appendix		107
	The Emerged Liturgy of the Palos Heights Christian Reformed Church	
Bibliography		120

Preface

For eighteen months I enjoyed the privilege of participating in a colloquy on Reformed worship sponsored by the Institute of Reformed Theology, an agency of the Union Theological Seminary and Presbyterian School of Christian Education (Union-PSCE). It provided a splendid opportunity to talk about worship with about thirty Reformed Christians from around the country. This group of scholars included pastors, professors, and church professionals from the Presbyterian Church (USA), the Reformed Church in America, and the Christian Reformed Church in North America. We met on five occasions over two years, including three times on the campus of Calvin College, and once each on the campuses of Hope College in Holland, Michigan and of the Union-PSCE in Richmond, Virginia.

During our final session we touched on the "great divide" between theory and practice. In preparation for that meeting, I attempted to identify principles essential to the worship of Reformed people. I submitted a document to my peers for their review. This publication represents the maturation of that discussion. In it I identify and commentate upon biblical principles that shape, to one degree or another, the weekly gathering of God's people.

I have written this document as a resident pastor. In other words, I write from the trenches, not from the halls of academia. I have had the privilege of teaching theology on college or university campuses, but, at this point of my life, I am serving in the pastorate where I have the privilege of planning and leading worship in a particular place at a particular time with a particular people. Now, I don't have the luxury of only pontificating about the current state of worship in American Protestantism; I am part of the problem and, hopefully, part of the solution.

I am a Minister of the Word and Sacraments in the Christian Reformed Church in North America (CRCNA), a denomination with roots in the Netherlands. It is an immigrant denomination. While it has been in the United States for 150 years, few congregations in the CRCNA have effectively settled in their communities, by which I mean, they fail to reflect the demographic makeup of those communities. Most of our congregations include a good number of "Dutch" folk. Consequently, when we measure diversity, we do so, not by the number of people of color, but by the number of non-Dutchmen.

For nine years, I have had the privilege of serving the Palos Heights Christian Reformed Church, a congregation of over eight hundred souls. This fifty-year-old community of believers gathers each week at a facility in a relatively small southwest suburb of Chicago, Illinois, called "Palos Heights" (12,000 residents). Economically, we are a predominantly middle-to-upper class congregation. Demographically, we are WASPs – White Anglo-Saxon Protestants. Sociologically, we serve a community that includes two colleges. As a result, our worshiping congregation includes many academicians and students, but an equal number of truck drivers and trades people.

Observers may describe our congregation as both Reformed and Evangelical. Our theological roots sink deep into the sixteenth-century, to the groundbreaking work of John Calvin. We are Calvinists who love to sing of God's grace. For us, salvation is all about God's unconditional love. When it comes to worship, we focus on the sermon which, for us, is the proclaimed Word of God. We also believe that God has called us, not to withdraw from the world, but to transform it for Jesus Christ. Our hope is to submit every nook and cranny of creation to the sovereign will of God in Christ.

We are also Evangelicals. We live within air waves of the Moody Bible Institute and Olivet Nazarene University whose radio programs are welcomed in nearly every member's home. In addition, televised mega-church pastors enter many homes through the medium of cable or satellite television. Furthermore, the booming "Christian" publication industry has produced countless "evangelical" products that have been purchased and read by my members. Consequently, the spirit of evangelicalism has seeped into our very being, to the dismay of some.

Observers may describe our weekly gathering or liturgy in any number of ways, but the best word may be "emerging." I would not have thought that word appropriate until I read Dan Kimball's description of "emerging worship," found in his book by that same title.[1] Like that model, our worship services call for maximum participation by the worshipers, utilize the gifts of those gathered, take place in sacred space, are multi-sensory, encourage freedom of movement, include sacraments and other historic forms, emphasize prayer, and are Christ-centered. The principles in this volume will help the reader understand how we arrived in such a place.

I am the sixth pastor of the Palos Heights Christian Reformed Church, and the first one who was not trained at the Calvin Theological Seminary in Grand Rapids, Michigan. I came in through the "back door," after twenty years of ministry in our sister denomination, the Reformed Church in America. I have been blessed with diverse biblical and theological training. I was raised in the Christian Reformed Church, where I memorized much of the Heidelberg Catechism as a youth. I attended a Church of Christ college where my Calvinistic moorings were shaken, but not dismantled. I continued my academic training at Wheaton Graduate School, McCormick Theological Seminary, and Marquette University. If I had to pick a label, I would choose Evangelical Reformed, but that label fails to convey my appreciation for both the Confessional and Charismatic movements.

As a resident pastor, I have been given the privilege of planning and leading the worship of God's people for over twenty-five years. In that role I have attempted to be faithful to my Reformed convictions while remaining open to the contributions of American Evangelicalism. I am a Calvinist who, with the Evangelicals, accents the centrality of preaching, the authority and infallibility of Scripture, the call to bring the Gospel throughout the world, the necessity of a personal relationship with Jesus Christ, the priesthood of all believers, the gifting of the Holy Spirit, the importance of personal holiness, and an appreciation for free worship flowing from the ever-present power of the Holy Spirit. I am an Evangelical

---

[1] Dan Kimball, *Emerging Worship: Creating Worship Gatherings for New Generations* (Grand Rapids, MI: Zondervan Publishing Co, 2004), 74-95.

who appreciates the seventeenth-century Free Church tradition of England, a movement that protested against "formed worship" or the ecclesiastical mandate to use the Book of Common Prayer. I would rather participate in congregational song or listen to one person speak than engage a unison reading or responsive reading. Similarly, I prefer a personal testimony in word or song over a corporate unison profession with an ancient creed. For years I allowed my personal preferences to shape the worship of God's people. The services I crafted and led didn't differ much from those offered by my non-Calvinist Baptist friends down the road, except, in my opinion, they were better. From a marketing vantage point, I tried to compete on the "open market" with a generic order of worship. In the end, however, I orchestrated dissonant liturgies for God's people by indiscriminately embracing liturgical practices inconsistent with Scripture. That experience motivated this work.

I release this project for publication with reservation. The liturgy of a worshiping community is not like a construction project that begins with a ground breaking ceremony followed by a building dedication. Instead, it is like an organism that emerges from the soil. The liturgy reflects the ongoing interplay between a particular gathered community, the culture in which it lives, and, above all, the prompting of our Triune God. Consequently, while the main parts remain the same, there has been, and will continue to be, growth and development within the parts. It was John Nevin who reminded me that no liturgy has even been considered "to be of perpetual force, even for the particular country or province in which it was used." In other words, the Christian Church expects, even longs for its liturgies to change.

> The old Swiss Liturgies in this way changed. The old Liturgy of the Palatinate became antiquated, even in the Palatinate itself. There was a movement all along, in other words, towards the realization of something in worship, which it was felt had not been fully reached in existing forms.[2]

---

[2] John Williamson Nevin, "Historical Vindication of the New Liturgy," in *Catholic and Reformed: Selected Theological Writings of John Williamson Nevin*, edited by Charles Yrigoyen, Jr. and George H. Bricker (Pittsburgh, PA: The Pickwick Press, 1978), 317.

Nevin believed that the longing for "satisfactory liturgies" flows from a "deeper consciousness of the Church" that "refuses to settle into contentment" with modern innovations.[3] Such is the case in my life and that of my congregation.

    I also release this project in a spirit of thanksgiving. I thank the Lord for the privilege of serving the Palos Heights Christian Reformed Church, a wonderful community of believers that has blessed me more than I could ever bless them. I thank the Lord for the Institute of Reformed Theology, and for the friendships developed through the colloquy. I thank the Lord for those members of the colloquy and congregation who provided invaluable insight and feedback during the development of this publication, especially the Reverend Robert Johnson. Finally, I thank the Lord for His amazing grace without which I, a ragamuffin, would be on a hopeless road to no where.

---

[3] John Williamson Nevin, "Historical Vindication of the New Liturgy," 318.

Introduction

**Principle #1 On the Regulative Principle:
Worship is Principle Driven.**

When a young man "falls in love," his heart filled with awe, he expresses love for his beloved through words or actions. Not wanting to convey the wrong impression, he initiates an investigation. He talks to friends and family members of his beloved to learn her longings, preferences, and desires. It would be disastrous, for example, to offer her a box of chocolate if she is a diabetic. In his research the young man discovers that his beloved enjoys roses. So, after a trip to a money machine, he picks up and delivers a dozen roses. The response of the beloved is everything he had hoped for.

That illustration from the everyday lives of lovers teaches us an important principle: the beloved determines whether or not a gift from the lover constitutes love. That simple principle helps worship planners realize that the beginning place for any discussion about how we worship is God. Since we desire to love our Triune God through worship, we first seek to learn His heart. If we hope that our contrived forms of adoration will constitute loving acts of devotion, we first seek God's preferences for our worship.

We begin our search in the written Word of God where we discover many wrong ways to worship God, most notably, through the use of graven

Introduction

images. While searching, however, we do not find a prescribed form of worship. We don't discover one liturgy for the Church, valid at all times and in all places. In its absence, we conclude that there is not one way of loving God through worship, "nor can there ever be."[1]

But that's not the end of our search. While the Scriptures do not provide a permanent order of worship for God's people, they do include several principles that reflect the heart of God for worship. These principles, then, guide our corporate response to the "gracious and redeeming act of God in Jesus Christ." This means, as Michael Horton points out, that "while one cannot point to a single liturgy and say that it contains the only form of genuine worship, some are clearly better than others."[2]

Some congregations choose to develop their worship services or liturgies upon other foundations than the principles revealed in Scripture. Some build purpose driven services. They determine, for example, that the purpose of the Sunday morning gathering is to reach the lost, and then develop a service that best accomplishes that objective. This approach has been developed masterfully by many "seeker-sensitive" congregations. Others develop market driven services. They survey a community, asking citizens, believers and un-believers alike, what they like or do not like about "church," and then develop a service sensitive to those responses. Still other congregations develop liturgies upon tradition, mimicking the worship of saints who have gone before them. And then there are those who follow the fads of the fastest growing churches, or the whims and preferences of whoever happens to be the key influencer or influencers within a congregation.

If we long to love the Lord through our worship, however, the best foundation for liturgical renewal is His revealed will. In other words, we want liturgies that emerge from biblical roots. Elsie McKee describes the two popular versions of the regulative principle: "All the Reformers agreed that nothing in worship may contradict Scripture, and some went further and made Scripture the paradigm for right worship."[3] One version of the

---

[1] Howard Hageman, *Pulpit and Table* (Richmond, Virginia: John Knox Press, 1962), 124.
[2] Michael Horton, *A Better Way: Rediscovering the Drama of Christ-Centered Worship* (Grand Rapids, MI: Baker Book House, 2002), 142.
[3] Elsie Anne McKee, "Reformed Worship in the Sixteenth Century," *Christian Worship in Reformed Churches Past and Present*, edited by Lukas Vischer (Grand Rapids, MI: Eerdmans Publishing Co, 2003), 8.

regulative principle, then, states that we should only worship in a manner that has direct sanction from God's Word. In support of this view, the Westminster Confession states that the church cannot go beyond God's revealed will in worship. Faithful to that historic confession, Edmund Clowney writes, "The church has authority to order worship, but not to introduce new elements beyond those that God has provided." He adds:

> The church, in its rightful sphere of authority, may order worship. But ordering worship activities that the Lord approves is not the same as adding those that he has not approved, especially since participation in public worship is not optional.[4]

A second, and more popular version of the regulative principle follows the conviction that the Bible does not contain an order for worship, a comprehensive directory for worship, or parameters for worship practice in every time and place. Instead, it offers biblical or theological principles that should shape the worship of God's people. Lukas Vischer writes,

> In Scripture we encounter a community responding to the living God, and we are called to associate ourselves to this response. The pattern of the response will not at all times and places be the same. God meets us where we are, and we respond out of our particular situation; and always and everywhere, God is present and speaks to us through word and sacrament, in the community of faith, and we – the gathered community – communicate with God in prayer.[5]

Personally, I affirm the second view of the regulative principle. I conclude that since the Bible does not provide a liturgy or detailed instructions for conducting worship, God would have us discern biblical and theological principles to shape our worship. When that happens, each of our liturgical actions will have biblical support and nothing in worship

---

[4] Edmund P. Clowney, *The Church* (Downers Grove, IL: InterVarsity Press, 1995), 120-123.
[5] Lukas Vischer, *Christian Worship in Reformed Churches Past and Present* (Grand Rapids, MI: Eerdmans Publishing Co, 2003), 282.

Introduction

will contradict scripture. Furthermore, while I cannot disagree with the logic of those who hold the first view, I don't believe it consistent with the active role of the Holy Spirit, nor with personal experience, nor with the consensus of the faithful. In other words, my reality contradicts the logic of the view that we can only worship in ways explicitly mandated by Scripture.

My reality also tells me, however, that more than we care to admit, our worship fails to match our biblical and theological convictions. Too often I experience inconsistency between principle and practice. Here is an example. In one year I received, or witnessed, six invitations to rise from my seat, come forward and, thereby, declare my intent to believe in or recommit my life to Jesus Christ. The invitations came in diverse settings but shared several commonalities. Each followed a stirring biblical message that included a concise presentation of the Gospel. Each included an opportunity to rise from my seat and walk to a predetermined location to receive further instruction. This activity was described, in each case, as a necessary method by which I could move closer to Christ or make a decision for Christ. Finally, and most importantly for this discussion, each one received the enthusiastic support of Reformed Christians who subscribe to a Calvinistic doctrine of sin and salvation.

The broad based support of altar calls by modern Reformed Christians surprised me. For the past 150 years most American Calvinists have refused to adopt such a decisionist technique. They found the practice inconsistent with Reformed theology.[6] That is not to suggest that God limits His work in the world to that which is consistent with such an understanding of God's Word. I have heard believers testify to God's work in their lives through the work of a faithful evangelist who proclaimed the Gospel with power and then called them forward as a testimony to their faith in the shed blood of Jesus. Nor is it to say that we should withhold support from evangelists or agencies that employ decisionist techniques. With Paul we may choose to be content that the Gospel of Christ is proclaimed.

The surprise relationship between Reformed Christians and decisionist techniques, however, raises the question of the relationship between principle and practice. Shouldn't we expect the worship service

---

[6] See Sam Hamstra, Jr., "Altar Calls and Effectual Calls," *Modern Reformation* (July/August 1998), 19-22.

of a gathered community to reflect its creeds and confessions? Of course! We expect those responsible for planning worship to order services that harmonize with their theologies. We expect them to reject liturgical innovations inconsistent with their congregation's biblical convictions? By failing to do so, they potentially divorce the minds of worshipers from their hearts. In the end, worshipers who share religious experiences without biblical moorings fail, as Marva Dawn notes, to grow in the grace and knowledge of the Lord.[7]

This book has been designed for those responsible for planning the weekly worship service of God's people. It identifies biblical principles that, to one degree or another, shape the weekly gathering of every local congregation of Christians. It articulates principles that guide the formation of a congregation's liturgical life, that help worship planners discern between the genuine and the spurious, between "what is abiding and what is ephemeral."[8] Paul Fremont captures what I hope would be the experience of every person or group planning worship while thinking biblical and theologically:

> They will creatively stretch outward from the edges. They will preserve the old without resisting the new. They will be characterized by an opening outwards, an unfolding of creative and meaningful new praxis and forms. They will have a firm grasp of their core beliefs and values, and will operate out of a strongly theological framework. Their life will be less about perpetuating trendiness, about being 'trendy', and more about integrity, faithfulness, authenticity, and relational depth.[9]

Before proceeding through a review of the biblical roots that shape emerging liturgies, I offer one clarification on the word "liturgy." If you are an "Evangelical," you may not like the term "liturgy." It "may seem like a dirty word… suggesting the Roman Catholic mass or the Episcopalian

---

[7] Marva J. Dawn, *Reaching Out Without Dumbing Down: A Theology of Worship for the Turn-Of-The-Century Culture* (Grand Rapids, MI: Eerdmans Publishing, Co., 1995).
[8] Donald G. Bloesch, *The Church: Sacraments, Worship, Ministry, Mission* (Downers Grove, IL: InterVarsity Press, 2002), 139.
[9] Paul Fremont, *Belonging and Not Belonging: The Creative Margins* (January 2, 2003).

Introduction

prayer book, accompanied by vestments, candles, and altars."[10] But the term "liturgy" should have more play among Evangelicals. The word derives from the Greek λειτουργια, transliterated as "leitourgia," a word that means "the work of the people." The word "liturgy" simply refers to the collection of components within a ceremony, ritual, or service. In other words, it refers to what Christians do when they gather each week. As one denominational report states:

> Every church has a liturgy, whether it worships with set forms inherited from the ages or whether it worships in the freedom of the moment. The only question is whether we have the best possible liturgy: it is never whether we have a liturgy.[11]

In this work, I use the word "liturgy" in its broadest, yet simplest application: to refer to the work of the people that makes corporate worship possible. The liturgy provides the framework within which, or the tools by which, we worship our Triune God. Most important for this discussion, I believe that while worship prompts the creation of a liturgy and lies at its core, the liturgy properly includes elements which we do not usually consider acts of corporate worship. In other words, it includes our coming and going, as well as what we do once we are together.

As a Reformed Christian, this understanding of liturgy plays well with my conviction that "worship encompasses all of life and it is misleading to imagine it only as a corporate activity of the assembled church." We offer ourselves to God as living sacrifices (Romans 12:1). We work unto the Lord, even recreate unto the Lord. I use the word "liturgy," then, to refer specifically to our corporate worship, which is a "particular expression of a life of perpetual worship."[12]

---

[10] D.G. Hart & John R. Muether, *With Reverence and Awe: Returning to the Basics of Reformed Worship* (Phillipsburg, New Jersey: P&R Publishing, 2002), 92.
[11] This quote is from the "Liturgical Committee Report," *Acts of Synod of the Christian Reformed Church* (Grand Rapids, MI: Christian Reformed Church, 1968), 135-136.
[12] R. Kent Hughes in *Worship by the Book*, edited by D.A. Carson (Grand Rapids, MI: Zondervan Publishing Co., 2002), 139-140.

Chapter One
Our Triune God and Worship

**Principle #2 On the Initiative for Worship:
Worship begins with God.**

> *Praise the Lord! Praise the Lord all you peoples!*
> *From the rising of the sun to the place where it sets,*
> *the name of the Lord is to be praised! (Psalm 113)*

For one reason or another, we get out of bed on a Sunday morning and head off to a place called "church," where we gather with some people to worship the Lord. From our perspective, it seems like **we** decide to worship the Lord, but, then, the longer we are at it, the more we begin to understand that **God** draws us to worship Him. So, while it appears otherwise, we conclude that our worship begins, not with us, but with God.

The Bible teaches that God the Father who created us, God the Son who redeemed us, and God the Spirit solicit our worship in three ways. First, our Triune God has wired us for worship. Hughes Oliphant Old succinctly summarizes that biblical truth with these words:

> We worship because God created us to worship him. Worship is at the center of our existence, at the heart of our reason for being.[1]

The Westminster Short Catechism echoes Old's sentiment pronouncing that our purpose as humans, our "chief end," is "to glorify God and enjoy him forever." The apostle Paul argues this point in Romans 1:18-23 where he teaches us that every human being witnesses the invisible qualities of God in creation and should, therefore, worship Him, instead of worshiping idols. In other words, when we live as God created us to live, we witness how God's "glory shines over all the earth," we discover that His "love is higher than the heavens" and His "faithfulness reaches to the skies" (Psalm 108:4-5), and we glorify the Lord. As the Psalmist once sung,

> When I consider your heavens, the work of your fingers, the moon and the stars, which you have set in place, what is man that you are mindful of him, the son of man that you care for him?.. O Lord, our Lord, how majestic is your name in all the earth! (Psalm 8:3-4,9)

Clearly, "worship is not simply a good thing to do," as Thomas Long points out, but "a necessary thing to do to be human:"

> When all the clutter is cleared away from our lives, we human beings do not merely need to engage in corporate worship; we truly want to worship in communion with others. All of us know somewhere in our hearts that we are not whole without such worship, and we hunger to engage in that practice. Thus, planners of worship do not make worship meaningful; worship is already meaningful.[2]

Second, our Triune God initiates worship, not only by creating us for worship, but by re-creating us for worship. I believe it was A.W. Tozer who once said, "Christ came to make worshipers out of rebels." In other words, the Lord saved us from our sins, adopted us as his children,

---

[1] Hughes Oliphant Old, *Worship Reformed according to Scripture,*" (Louisville, KY: Westminster John Knox Press, 2002), 1.
[2] Thomas G. Long, *Beyond the Worship Wars: Building Vital and Faithful Worship* (The Alban Institute, 2003), 17.

and indwelt us with the Holy Spirit "to the praise of his glorious grace" (Ephesians 1:6). Lest we doubt the words of Paul, the apostle Peter echoed his teaching with these words: "You are a people who belong to God, that you may declare the praises of him who called you out of darkness into his wonderful light" (I Peter 2:9).

We witness the relationship between salvation and worship throughout the Scriptures, but particularly in the narratives surrounding Christ's birth. Each person or angel who heard the Gospel message praised the Lord. Mary sang, "My soul magnifies the Lord and my spirit rejoices in God my Savior" (Luke 1:46-47). An angel of the Lord joined a great company of the heavenly host and praised the Lord (Luke 2:9-12). Astrologers from the East found Jesus and worshiped Him (Matthew 2:11). From those testimonies and others we may conclude that God saved us to worship Him. Walt Wangerin captures that conviction with this prayer:

> O Lord, you are the musician, and we are all your instruments. You breathe, and we come to life. You breathe, and we are horns for your glory. You blow through the winds of the spirit, and we like chimes cannot keep silent. You pluck the strings of our hearts, and we become a psalm. You come, and we must sing.[3]

Even now, we, who have been saved by grace, delight in the presence of our Savior and glory in the beauty of His holiness. Those impulses will remain with us through eternity when, with all the angels and saints, we will worship the Lord singing, "Praise and glory and wisdom and thanks and honor and power and strength be to our God for ever and ever" (Revelation 7:12).

Until Christ comes again, sin derails God's plan for us. Consequently, instead of worshiping the Lord, we worship ourselves. Influenced by the ever-present power of sin, we enjoy the blessings of the created world and the comforts of our redemption while failing to worship God, the giver of every good and perfect gift. For that reason the Lord has not only created and re-created us for worship, he has also commanded us to worship Him.

---

[3] Walter Wangerin, Jr., *Preparing for Jesus* (Grand Rapids, MI: Zondervan Publishing House, 1999), 82.

Principled Worship

Scripture includes numerous mandates to worship the Lord, many of which may be found in the Psalms. In Psalm 113, for example, we read,

> Praise the Lord! Praise the Lord all you peoples! From the rising of the sun to the place where it sets, the name of the Lord is to be praised!

God's mandate corrects any and all self-centered approaches to worship. It reminds us that we don't gather with God's people to have our needs met, or to feel better, or to "get something out of it." Worship is not about us; it is about obedience. If we didn't get a thing out of it, we would still worship the Lord, responding to His grace and grandeur with adoration.

The principle that God initiates worship dramatically shapes how the worship leader, liturgist, or pastor frames corporate worship. Once the community has gathered, the worship leader, for example, will undoubtedly greet the corporate body. His or her words may convey a couple truths. First, they may extend hope for the time spent together. Traditionally, these words of hope have been referred to as "sentences" or "votum." As a child our pastor began the service with "Our help is in the name of the Lord who made the heavens and the earth." Those words set the stage for that which was to follow. It marked us as hope-filled people dependent upon God.

Unfortunately, some worship leaders greet the gathered community as if it is a PTA meeting. They begin with a generic "Good Morning," words we hear from the morning network news crew. But why say "Good Morning" when we can say so much more? Those who respond to God's call have chosen to leave a world of meaningless "Good Mornings" for but an hour or more with God's people. They have made that choice, in part, because they long to be greeted with hope. They want to be assured that, during their time together, they will receive the grace of God, be reminded of the love of God, and experience fellowship with the Holy Spirit.

Second, the greeting may acknowledge the ecclesiastical authority that has sanctioned the gathering. A former professor once asked, "Who are you to welcome me to worship? It's not your service." He was right. The pastor doesn't have the authority to stand before a congregation and welcome them to participation in the liturgy. The service does not belong to the pastor, worship leader or liturgist. The liturgy is the corporate response of God's people to God's call. In a day and age when worship quickly turns to entertainment, and worship leaders sound more and more like stand-up comedians or disc-jockeys, we may properly shape the attitude of the gathered community by identifying the authority by which we speak and worship. I suggest that minimally, and most importantly, we welcome the gathered community in the name of Jesus Christ, the head of the Church.

After the "greeting," the liturgist calls God's people to worship. This action shifts the attention of the congregants to the triune God. It moves hearts and minds to a bigger stage. It paves the way for a spirit of "reverence and awe" among the congregation (Hebrews 12:28). The "Call to Worship" may take many forms as long as it accomplishes those simple goals. It may be spoken by one person. It may be spoken by the worshiping community in unison, responsively, or antiphonally. Personally, I employ Scripture verses, believing that the implementation of ancient words speaks volumes about the role and priority of the Scriptures in the life of a congregation. Among other messages, the use of Scripture affirms our identity as a counter-cultural community with a unique vocabulary. My favorite Psalm is numbered 113. In fact, I begin nearly every Sunday morning worship service with these words: "Praise the Lord! Praise, O servants of the Lord, praise the name of the Lord! Let the name of the Lord be praised from the rising of the sun to the place where it sets, the name of the Lord is to be praised." Whatever words we use, may our calls to worship convey the biblical truth that God initiates our worship.

Principle #3 On the Potential for Worship
The Holy Spirit makes worship possible.

> *"In Christ, you are being built together to become a dwelling in which God lives by the Spirit." (Ephesians 2:22)*

At one time or another, you have been part of a civic, gathered community, that is, a group of people gathered in one room for one particular purpose. Perhaps you had that experience as a member of a Parent Teacher Association (PTA), or as a Veteran of Foreign Wars (VFW), or as a member of a political party. We participate in those kinds of gatherings because we believe that they bear a kind of fruit that can not be produced by isolated individuals. We understand that there is a unique power or potential that arises within a gathered community.

To a casual observer, the weekly gathering of Christians may appear similar in nature to a political rally where partisans display their placards and chant their slogans. But much more goes on. We believe that each gathered community is a temple of the Holy Spirit (I Corinthians 3:16) and that every believer is a temple of the Holy Spirit (I Corinthians 6:19). Furthermore, each believer is gifted by that same Spirit for service in the name of the Lord (I Corinthians 12:7).[4] The Heidelberg Catechism describes that charismatic work as the anointing of Christ, our chief prophet, only high priest, and eternal king.[5] Through the work of the Holy Spirit, every believer, as a priest, may confidently approach the throne of grace in prayer (Hebrews 4:16); every believer, as a prophet, must be prepared to defend the faith; and every believer, as a king, may exercise his or her spiritual gifts and, thereby, extend the reign of Christ in the world. As Leslie Newbigin writes,

> To be in Christ is to share in His anointing, to have that Spirit by whom the word was made flesh and by whom the incarnate Word was anointed that He might fulfill the mission for which He was sent; it is to have "an anointing from the Holy One." And this anointing is nothing doubtful or debatable; on the contrary, it is the sure fact upon which we can rest our confidence that we are in Him and He is in us: "Hereby we know that he abideth in us, by the Spirit which he gave us (I John 3:24).[6]

In our not too distant past, we divided Christians into two groups: clergy and laity. That false distinction, left over from the Middle Ages, limited the leadership of worship to the ordained clergy which, as Hans Küng so aptly noted, allowed worship to "petrify into mediocrity and uniformity."[7] Today, with Abraham Kuyper and others, we affirm that "in Christ's Church there are not merely a few officials and a mass of idle,

---

[4] Jürgen Moltmann, *The Source of Life: The Holy Spirit and the Theology of Life*, (Minneapolis, MN: Augsburg Fortress Press, 1997), 97.
[5] Heidelberg Catechism Lord's Day 12.
[6] Leslie Newbigin, *The Household of God* (New York: Friendship Press, 1953), 99.
[7] Hans Küng, *The Church* (New York: Doubleday & Company, Inc., 1976), 249.

unworthy subjects."[8] The local church is a charismatic fellowship gifted by the Holy Spirit for its ministry in the name of Jesus Christ. The apostle writes, for example, that the Spirit has gifted some as pastors and teachers "so that the body of Christ may be built up until we all reach unity in the faith and in the knowledge of the Son of God and become mature, attaining to the whole measure of the fullness of Christ" (Ephesians 4:12). The Holy Spirit also empowers believers with gifts of leadership and encouragement, while gifting others with creative gifts that find fulfillment in the liturgy of God's people.

We may conclude, then, that "Christian worship is inspired by the Spirit, empowered by the Spirit, directed by the Spirit, purified by the Spirit, and bears the fruit of the Spirit."[9] Worship is a gift (a charism) of God to God's people. As such, it is filled with promise, not because of what we bring to worship, but because of the promised presence of the Holy Spirit.

Were it not for the Holy Spirit, we could not hope for much of anything to happen in worship. That's because we come to worship with spiritual senses impaired by sin. Even though we have been born again, we often hear what we want to hear and see what we want to see. Add to that the unfortunate truth that our cold hearts, stubborn wills, and closed minds too often choose to hinder the work of the Spirit in our lives, an action Paul describes as "grieving the Spirit" (Ephesians 4:30). If we doubt our spiritual limitations, we need but review the tainted history of the Christian church. In its tattered past, we will discover professing Christians committing heinous atrocities in the name of the Lord. And, were it not for grace, we could do the same.

Thankfully, God the Spirit presides with the gathered community. God the Spirit convicts us of sin and guides us into truth (John 16:5-15), brings light into our darkness so that we may see the glory of God in the face of Jesus Christ (II Corinthian 4:6), encourages our weary hearts, and quenches our thirsty souls. Because of the promised presence of the Holy Spirit, we attend worship expecting nothing less than a meaningful encounter with God or, as Dallas Willard wrote, a "purposive interaction

---

[8] Abraham Kuyper, *The Work of the Holy Spirit,* translated by Henri De Vries (Grand Rapids, MI: Eerdmans Publishing Co., 1979), 183.
[9] Hughes Oliphant Old, *Worship Reformed according to Scripture,* 5.

with the grace of God in Christ."[10] John Calvin describes that expectation as "a living moment proceeding from the Holy Spirit, where the heart is righteously touched, and the understanding illumined."[11] When we come together, then, even with all of our spiritual limitations, we hope that the Holy Spirit - not the preacher or the music or the liturgy - will mysteriously, freely, and unpredictably touch our hearts, minds and wills.

Of course, while we may assume the Spirit's presence with the gathered community, we may never presume its blessing. The Spirit works freely and sovereignly, blowing where and when it wills. So, even though the Scriptures assure us that the Spirit presides with the gathered community, we still plead with the Holy Spirit to bless us for "unless the living Spirit Himself takes the things of Christ and shows them to us, we can not know them."[12] On one hand, then, we don't have to create an atmosphere, perhaps through corporate singing, that entices the Holy Spirit to join our service in such a way that we feel its presence. The Holy Spirit is present whether we feel it or not. On the other hand, through our prayers we will ask, seek and knock for the Spirit's blessing upon us. Like the neighbor in Christ's parable who made a nuisance of himself, we will keep calling until the Lord blesses us.

Typically, we solicit the Spirit's blessing through two prayers: the "Invocation" and the "Prayer for Illumination." Through the "Invocation" we do not invoke the Spirit's presence. Instead, we acknowledge our limitations and ask the Spirit to work in such a way that the "words of our lips and the meditations of our hearts" may be acceptable to our Triune God. Through the "Prayer for Illumination" we, once again, acknowledge our human limitations but, then, seek the illuminating grace of the Holy Spirit upon the reading and preaching of the Word. We seek the Spirit's light in our darkness. We may offer this prayer at the outset of the service, or as a special petition before the reading of Scripture and the proclamation of the Word.

---

[10] Dallas Willard, *Renovation of the Heart: Putting on the Character of Christ* (Colorado Springs, CO: NavPress, 2002), 22-23.

[11] This quote is from an unpublished translation by Robert Johnson of John Calvin's preface to his 1542 "Form of Prayers and Ecclesiastical Chants With the Manner of Administering the Sacraments and of Solemnizing Marriage According to Customs of the Ancient Church."

[12] Leslie Newbigin, *The Household of God*, 101.

In the last half of the twentieth-century, the Charismatic movement has prompted Reformed Christians to re-evaluate the extent of the Spirit's gracious work by highlighting the possibility of experiencing the "extra-ordinary" gifts of the Holy Spirit in worship. By that designation, I refer to those spiritual gifts labeled by the apostle Paul as tongues, prophecy, interpretation, and healing (I Corinthians 12:7-11). Typically, most Christians embrace unreservedly the spiritual gifts historically labeled "ordinary," but believe that the "extra-ordinary" gifts no longer have a place in the liturgies of God's people. Abraham Kuyper summarizes that traditional position:

> The charismata now existing in the Church are those pertaining to the ministry of the Word; the ordinary charismata of increased exercise of faith and love; those of wisdom, knowledge, and discernment of spirits; that of self-restraint; and lastly, that of healing the sick suffering from nervous and psychological diseases. The others for the present are inactive.[13]

Several non-Charistmatic types, denominationally speaking, have begun to question that conclusion. They have worshiped with Christians who practice the "extra-ordinary" gifts in their liturgies. During worship, for example, they have heard gifted individuals speak in tongues and other gifted individuals interpret those tongues. They have reflected on those experiences and concluded that there are only three biblical options. First, the "gifts" are a result of mental defect. In other words, the babblers and hallucinators are out of their minds. Second, the gifts are real but empowered by Satan. Third, the gifts flow from the Holy Spirit as promised in Scripture.

I opt for the third, first and foremost, because scripture supports it. One has to hop and skip through the teaching of Paul to conclude that some gifts were not meant to continue after the apostles. Plus, such a conviction becomes self-fulfilling. If a congregation doesn't expect the extra-ordinary gifts, it surely will not seek them. I agree with Donald Bloesch who, speaking within the mainstream of the Christian tradition, writes,

---

[13] Abraham Kuyper, *The Work of the Holy Spirit*, 188-189.

Principled Worship

I contend that all of the charisms belong to the wider ministry of the church in every generation. Some have fallen into eclipse, but not because the gifts have ceased with the passing of the apostolic church. Rather, through its desire to control, the church has grieved and quenched the Spirit so that the Spirit's distribution of the gifts has been impeded.... The Holy Spirit is conservative in the distribution of his gifts. He grants light only to those who demonstrate by their action that they need light. He gives strength only to those who are exhausting themselves in the struggle to do God's will."[14]

---

[14] Donald Bloesch, *The Holy Spirit: Works and Gifts*, (Downers Grove, IL: InterVarsity Press, 2000), 294.

Chapter Two
The Person Who Worships

**Principle #4 On the Heart of Worship:
Without love, our worship is nothing.**

> *"If I speak in the tongues of men and of angels, but have not love, I am only a resounding gong or a clanging cymbal. If I have the gift of prophecy and can fathom all mysteries, but have not love, I am nothing." (I Corinthians 13:1-2)*

Unusual, unique, peculiar, spectacular events catch our attention. That explains, in part, the current roster of television programs. Aware of our insatiable appetite for that which is out of the ordinary, television producers provide a smorgasbord of alternatives. We may choose from an ever growing list of talk shows. We may witness people airing dirty laundry in court before made-for-television judges. We may catch life as it happens by witnessing outlandish home videos. We may tune in to programs tagged "reality," which have about as much reality as professional wrestling.

We enjoy the unique. That desire, in itself, does not appear to be wrong. By it we stand enthralled before the Grand Canyon, we witness with amazement the birth of a baby, and we worship our one, holy, true God. Yet, our appreciation for the sensational and spectacular, if embraced without discretion, scrambles our priorities, stirs dissension, and, like a virus, weakens the body of Christ. That's what happened in Corinth.

The First Christian Church in Corinth enjoyed several spectacular manifestations of the Holy Spirit. Some Corinthians spoke the language of the Spirit. Others had faith like that of the apostles, a faith that enabled them to lead a struggling congregation with hope and confidence. Still others spoke the Word of God with power to an infant church in need of direction. Some were even encouraged to sacrifice their lives for the advancement of the Gospel. Like typical human beings, the Corinthians embraced the spectacular. But they went further. Without respect for the state of their souls, they treated those with gifts of tongues, prophecy, and knowledge like celebrities without whom the church could not survive. They lifted up the extra-ordinarily gifted to places of honor and glory. Consequently, the church was divided, not only into those who favored the preacher Apollos over the apostle Paul, but into the haves and the have-nots, the famous and not-so-famous, the essentials and non-essentials.

The apostle Paul, like a doctor, diagnosed the condition of the congregation and prescribed a remedy. He challenged the Corinthian's preoccupation with the spectacular gifts, and prescribed the greatest gift of all - love. Of course, they did not view love as the greatest. It seemed so mundane, so normal. Most important for this discussion, the Corinthians failed to appreciate love's unique contribution to corporate worship. So Paul wrote or borrowed a poem that described loves power. In it he even claimed that, without love, prominent liturgical actions were null and void. Jonathan Edwards aptly summarized Paul's teaching:

> The greatest blessing...in this world: greater than any natural gifts, greater than the greatest natural abilities, greater than any acquired endowments of mind, greater than the most universal learning, greater than any outward wealth and honor, greater than to be a king or an emperor, greater than to be taken as a shepherd and made a king like David; greater than all the riches and honor and magnificence of Solomon, in all his glory is love!... (Love) is the most glorious work of the Holy Spirit in the Church of Jesus Christ, more glorious, far more glorious, than a pouring out of the miraculous gifts of the Spirit..... This glory is

the greatest glory of the Church of Christ, and the greatest glory which Christ's Church will ever enjoy in any period.[1]

Paul's teaching on love corrects our pre-occupation with the spectacular: the great preacher, the great singer, the great healer, the great this, or the great that. It contests our tendency to accept, even prioritize the external without regard for the internal. Passionate preaching, excellent music, sacrificial service, generous contributions, solid doctrine, and a numerically growing congregation are wonderful blessings if and when they flow from grateful, humble, loving hearts. If they do not, they are like a diamond necklace that enhances the beauty of a woman, but does not enrich her soul.

Here is the question we face: Do we build our corporate life on the truth "that the ordinary influence of the Spirit of God, working the grace of love in our hearts, is a more excellent blessing than any of the extraordinary gifts of the Spirit?"[2] God blessed Moses as a prophet, David as a poet and king, Elijah as a prophet, Daniel as an interpreter of dreams, the apostles as miracles workers, and Paul as an evangelist. Yet, the gift of love is greater than the gifts of prophecy, tongues, miracles, and preaching. The Church of Christ in whom the Holy Spirit works the grace of love, is far more greatly blessed than any prophet, king, or apostle. If we believe that love is the greatest, then let us, as Jonathan Edwards exhorts,

> Earnestly seek this blessed fruit of the Spirit, and let us seek that it may abound in our souls; that the love of God may more and more be shed abroad in our hearts; and that we may love the Lord Jesus Christ in sincerity, and love one another as Christ hath loved us. (Then) we shall possess the richest of all treasures, and the highest and most excellent of all graces.[3]

Let us be honest, here. Corporate worship does not always provide a loving environment. We have too often found it convenient to divorce

---

[1] Jonathan Edwards, *Charity and Its Fruit*, (Carlisle, PA: Banner of Truth Trust, 1978), 43 & 46.
[2] Jonathan Edwards, *Charity and Its Fruit*, 30.
[3] Jonathan Edwards, *Charity and Its Fruit*, 321-322.

love from worship. Preachers speak with bitterness or anger in their souls. Congregants criticize every aspect of a service. Church members express love for God while withholding love for the persons sitting beside them. Guests come and go from gathered communities without receiving hospitality.

Replay our conversations about worship and we implicate ourselves. Countless books have been written about worship but few, if any, speak of love. That reality suggests that we have convinced ourselves that we will discover more effective and meaningful worship if we can only get a better preacher, a more creative liturgy, a more upbeat band, more advanced technology, or more user-friendly space. The Bible teaches, however, that the soil from which effective worship grows is love. Hence, the heart of the person who worships must be graced by love.

In his love poem, the apostle Paul identified one quality of love especially needed today: "love does not insist on its own way." The loving Christian doesn't come to worship thinking first and foremost about his or her needs, and then leave the sanctuary pouting when those needs are not met. Love, like a good host or hostess, seeks the good of others. John Powell wrote, "Love challenges me to break the fixation I have with myself...Love demands that I learn how to focus my attention on the needs of those I love."[4]

Therein lies the hope for peace that ends all worship wars. Therein also lies the hope for a contagious corporate life that, by God's grace, influences that "little part of the world we touch." When love characterizes our gatherings, we may hope that God's love will overflow into our neighborhoods. We may hope, as Walter J. Burghardt wrote, that "Someone will experience (life) with fresh eyes, will listen to Christ with ears open, will feel the touch of God, will find truth and beauty and goodness in a world that seemed desperately bleak and empty."[5]

---

[4] John Powell, *Unconditional Love,* (Allen, TX: Thomas More Publishing, 1978), 92.
[5] Walter Burghardt, *Sir, We Would Like To See Jesus,* (New York: Paulist Press, 1982), 85-86.

The Person Who Worships

Principle #5 On the Attitude of the Worshiper: The praise of God leads to confession of sin.

> *"I saw the Lord seated on a throne, high and exalted....*
> *'Woe to me!' I cried. 'I am ruined!*
> *For I am a person of unclean lips!'" (Isaiah 6:1,5)*

The worship of God in spirit and in truth has a domino effect. First, we encounter anew God's majesty and holiness. This experience, in turn, accents our deficiencies. In other words, the light of God's grandeur illumines our shortcomings. Once again, we see ourselves as God sees us. John Calvin writes,

> It is certain that a man never achieves clear knowledge of himself unless he has first looked upon God's face, and then descends from contemplating him to scrutinize himself. For we always seem to ourselves righteous and upright and wise and holy – this pride is innate in all of us... As long as we do not look beyond the earth, being quite content with our own righteousness, wisdom, and virtue, we flatter ourselves most sweetly, and fancy ourselves all but demigods.[6]

It is for that reason Jonathan Edwards referred to the proper attitude of the worshiper as "evangelical humility." He believed that the true worship of God not only convicts the conscience, but produces a "change of inclination affecting the whole self."[7] It transforms the worshiper into a seeker, receptive to the transforming work of the Holy Spirit. It puts us where our loving Lord wants us to be: in a place of humble dependence, with open arms to receive His grace.

The prophet Isaiah illustrates the inseparable connection between an encounter with God and confession of sin. After he faced the glory of God, Isaiah cried out, "I am ruined, for I am a man of unclean lips, and I live among a people of unclean lips, and my eyes have seen the King, the Lord God Almighty" (Isaiah 6:5). Like Isaiah, a genuine encounter with

---

[6] John Calvin, *Institutes of the Christian Religion*, I.1.ii.
[7] Jonathan Edwards, *Religious Affections*, in *The Works of Jonathan Edwards, Volume 2*, edited by John E. Smith (New Haven, CT: Yale University Press, 1959), 35.

the glory of God through worship creates the conviction of sin and, then, draws us to the throne of grace where we hope to find forgiveness. Aware of our sinfulness, we seek help from the Lord whose grace is greater than our sin. With Isaiah, we want our guilt to be taken away and our "sin atoned for" (Isaiah 6:6-7).

Fresh from an encounter with God in worship, then, we desire, first and foremost, the grace of reconciliation. Marva Dawn writes, "The more we encounter the holy God in our worship, the more we will recognize our utter sinfulness and be driven to repentance."[8] Donald Bloesch concurs:

> Worship that is done in spirit and in truth will entail an encounter with the Holy, who includes and transcends moral goodness. A true encounter with the Holy precipitates a sense of awe in which we experience our helplessness and littleness before an almighty God.[9]

The liturgy, then, **must** include a prayer of confession. A liturgy without confession raises suspicion about the validity of the worship within the liturgy. What kind of worship fails to move worshipers to confess their sins? Surely, not worship informed by the truth of God's character. Furthermore, a liturgy without a prayer of confession has a hard time claiming to be "Reformed." John Calvin, for example, insisted on the inclusion of prayers of confession, as did the Second Helvetic Confession and the Westminster Confession.[10]

The prayer of confession may take one of several forms. We may sing it through the use of a hymn or read it in unison. We may offer a specific prayer in silence. We may confess our sins by proxy, affirming as our own the spoken prayer of the pastor or the prayer sung by the choir or soloist. When we pray we may assume a physical position of humility before the Lord. We may sit with bowed head, a medieval sign of submission to one's Lord. We may kneel before the Lord or we may follow the ancient custom of holding our hands flat together. Whatever our posture, it should reflect humble submission before the Lord.

---

[8] Marva J. Dawn, *Reaching Out Without Dumbing Down*, 90.
[9] Donald G. Bloesch, *The Church: Sacraments, Worship, Ministry, Mission*, 119.
[10] See Michael Horton, *A Better Way*, 153-154.

The Person Who Worships

Here it is fair to offer a critique. While I deeply appreciate the rise of a new genre of sacred music labeled "praise and worship," and view it as the fruit of a special outpouring of God's Spirit upon the church, I have discovered very few confessional songs in that genre. While I have not completed a scientific study, my experience suggests that the ratio of praise songs to confessional songs must be close to one hundred to one.

This has had a trickle down effect on Christian congregations. During a recent "field trip," I visited two different congregations one Sunday morning. Both were "seeker-sensitive" and employed "praise bands," as well as power-point technology. Both committed a significant amount of time in the liturgy (though they would never call it such) to the worship of God. Both limited their corporate song to "praise and worship" music. Neither service included a prayer of confession.

Why not? What kind of God did I worship whereby I could praise Him and not be drawn to confession of sin? Did I praise the Triune God or some figment of my imagination? The teaching of Scripture seems clear in this area. Saints who have come into the presence of God, have been brought to confession. Praise that accents the attributes of our Holy God, leads to confession of sin. A liturgy without such a prayer is simply incomplete.

In Christian worship, it is imperative that an announcement of the good news follows confession of sin. Traditionally, this element has been called "absolution." Once convicted of alienation from God, we need assurance of reconciliation. Once convinced of our sin, we need affirmation of our forgiveness through the finished work of Jesus Christ. More specifically, we need to hear the Gospel. Now is not the time for the liturgist or pastor to offer personal words of encouragement. We have sinned against the Lord and only a word from the Lord can assure us of forgiveness. So the worship leader, in the name of Jesus, reads a selection from God's Word that captures the good news of reconciliation. He or she offers a public declaration that Jesus Christ has forgiven our sins.

Jesus connects the assurance of forgiveness to worship in a conversation with a Pharisee named Simon (Luke 7:36-50). While dining in his home, a "woman who had lived a sinful life" cleaned Jesus' feet, kissed them, and anointed them with perfume. Simon's objection led Jesus to compare the actions of the woman to those of the Pharisee. Jesus noted that when he came to his home, Simon did not wash his feet or even greet him with a kiss, but the "sinful" woman kissed his feet incessantly. Jesus, then, explained to Simon that the woman "loved" Jesus because she had a profound conviction of sin and a deep assurance of forgiveness.

In the same way, the acknowledgment of sin, through a prayer of confession, coupled with assuring words of forgiveness, prompts loving praise to the Lord. According to Jesus, the acknowledgment of our perpetual disobedience and the reminder of God's rich mercy, prompts praise. It is important, then, for those planning worship to grant the worshiper an opportunity to respond with gratitude to the assurance of God's eternal love. There are many options. We may respond with a corporate "Amen" or "Hallelujah," read a Psalm, or sing a hymn of thanksgiving for the redemption that is ours in Christ. But we will not remain silent; we can't.

Principle #6 On the Involvement of the Worshiper: Worship involves the whole person.

"Love the Lord your God with all your heart, with all your soul, and with all your mind. This is the first and greatest commandment."
(Matthew 22:37-38)

I will never forget "Big John," a retired gentleman who sat in the back pew each Sunday, with his arms crossed and his eyes fixed on me, the man behind the pulpit. During my sermon, he never moved. Yet, after each service he said, "Good sermon, Pastor." Personally, I thought he was just being kind. I did not see any physical manifestations that would lead me to believe he enjoyed my sermons. He never smiled, grimaced, or nodded. He simply looked straight ahead with his burly eyebrows curled in seriousness.

I had pretty much written John off as "dead," until I went to a professional baseball game with a group of senior citizens from the church. I sat next to John and guess what? He watched the ball game the same way he sat in church. In fact, when a home run landed ten feet from his seat, he barely moved. Then, as we left the stadium he said, "Good game, Pastor!"

John taught me an important lesson: Do not pass judgment about the spiritual condition of a person's heart based on the way that person worships. He also taught me that, ideally, individual Christians will worship in a manner true to themselves. They will worship in a way consist with their complex personalities which uniquely blend three major elements: the cognitive (mind or intellect), the volitional (will), and the emotive (heart). Through casual observation, we notice that each individual's personality usually accents one element over another. In a congregation, some people are more emotive; they are the ones clapping their hands, raising their arms, and shouting "Amen." Some are more volitional and like to combine actions with their liturgical acts; they are they ones who stand to profess faith and kneel when they pray. Some are more cognitive; for them the liturgy comes through their eyes into the minds and then to the heart; they appreciate the visual and silence which prompt biblical reflection.

We face two challenges in this area. First, we struggle respecting those who worship in a manner different than our own. In other words, we expect uniformity of expression by our fellow worshipers. We reveal our expectations with our all too often sarcastic comments about worshipers in other traditions. We label Pentecostals as "happy clappers" or "holy-rollers." We have a habit of concluding that worshipers in Roman or Orthodox traditions are just "going through the motions." Comments like those reflect our desire for everyone to worship just like us.

Second, we struggle designing liturgies that involve the entire person: mind, body and heart. Most liturgies emphasize one part of the worshiper's personality, while neglecting the other two. I suggest that worship regulated by scripture will include the regular use of the emotive, volitional and cognitive components of our personhood. It will engage our hearts, minds and wills. In so doing, it will gently nudge people out of their comfort zones, not allowing them to worship with but one part of their being.

In my limited liturgical experience, primarily among Reformed, predominantly white, suburban congregations, I have found the volitional or emotive component of human nature minimized, if not eradicated, in favor of the cognitive or notional. Compared to my Roman Catholic and Orthodox friends, we don't have much liturgical action, except for the stand-up sit-down movements that frame congregational song and the recitation of the Apostles' Creed. Compared to my charismatic and

African American friends, we don't encourage the kinds of emotions that typically characterize confession of sin and celebration. We Reformed folk have adopted a predominantly cognitive approach to the liturgy. We worship by engaging our minds, and our minds alone, with God's Word, leading some from within, and many from without, to label us as the "frozen chosen."

While I deeply appreciate the richness of my liturgical tradition, as well as the benefits of a strong intellectual component in worship, I long for opportunities to worship the Lord with my entire being, especially my heart. I share the concern of Jonathan Edwards who concluded that a notional approach to worship often "leaves the individual soul outside as a spectator looking on at the feast."[11] Edwards asked, "Who can deny that true religion consists in a great measure in vigorous and lively actings of the inclination and will of the soul, or the fervent exercise of the heart?"[12] Presbyterian Jane Vann agrees by acknowledging that the "liturgy elicits from God's people a broad sweep of emotions," and by advocating the inclusion of the "spiritual affections" in worship.[13] The Psalmist leaves no room for debate with the following liturgical prescription:

> "Sing to the Lord!" "Clap your hands to the Lord!" "Kneel before the Lord your maker!" "Rejoice in the Lord!" "Humble yourself before the Lord!" "Praise Him with dancing!" "Lift up your hands in the sanctuary!"

For the Psalmist, worship is demonstrative: "it pours from your heart, it infuses your inclinations to please God, and it directs your will to serve him."[14] As N. T. Wright wrote, "When the ascended Lord comforts the disturbed and disturbs the comforted, the result is reckless adoration."[15]

---

[11] Jonathan Edwards, *Religious Affections,* 48.
[12] Jonathan Edwards, *Religious Affections,* 24.
[13] Jane Rogers Vann, *Gathered Before God: Worship-Centered Church Renewal* (Louisville, KY: John Knox Press, 2004), 68-69.
[14] R. Kent Hughes, "Free Church Worship: The Challenge of Freedom, in *Worship by the Book,* edited by D.A. Carson, Timothy Kelly, Mark Ashton, and R. Kent Hughes (Grand Rapids, MI: Zondervan, 2002), 161-162.
[15] N.T. Wright, *For All God's Worth: True Worship and the Calling of the Church,"* (Grand Rapids, MI: Eerdmans, Publishing, Co., 1997), 88.

Of course, some might find our emotion distasteful and disturbing, but that's all right.

> I suspect we all reach a point where somebody else's enthusiasm strikes us as over the top. But, let's face it, the whole point of enthusiasm is that it's over the top; and if you're not enthusiastic about Jesus, or are tempted to mock somebody who is, look around and see what company you're keeping.[16]

Principle #7 On the Offerings of the Worshiper: Worship includes offerings.

> *"On the first day of every week, each one of you should set aside a sum of money in keeping with his income." (I Corinthians 16:2)*

I was nurtured in the faith by an immigrant congregation, one that dictated minimal financial contributions for its own ministry so that its members might contribute more money to other Christian agencies. This is how it worked, as I remember it. Each year, the Council would carefully craft as skinny a budget as possible, knowing, all too well, that any increases would solicit indignation from a predictable number of congregants. Once approved by the congregation, the Council would divide the bottom line of the "Operating Budget" by the number of giving units or households in the congregation. Each unit was then asked to contribute the same amount each week to sustain the ministry of the congregation. The members were provided with pre-printed envelopes, one for each week, with which they would enclose their money (or "pay their budget"). When they arrived for worship, they would place their envelopes in a small, white, locked box located just inside the entrance to the building. During worship, then, the Deacons received an offering for a cause other than the "Budget." Looking back, I can say that that system of giving helped my immigrant congregation reach a very important goal: the building of a religious and cultural infrastructure in a foreign land. My forefathers and mothers were

---

[16] N.T. Wright, *For All God's Worth*, 88.

a generation of builders who left behind a handful of vibrant para-church agencies that have played a transformative role in the lives of many.

However, that system of giving includes several flaws. First, it did not have biblical precedent. Second, it did not prioritize giving to the local church. Hence, I don't think it an accident that our local para-church ministries flourished while our congregation failed to impact its community with the Gospel. Third, and most important for this discussion, it removed the financial support of the local church from worship. Intentionally or not, it turned that action into an obligation. That's why I grew up hearing fellow church members refer to their weekly contribution to the church as "paying the budget," words which conveyed to me an attitude far removed from gratitude.

The Scriptures, however, provide a different model, one that considers each of our financial gifts as acts of worship. In Genesis 14, for example, we read that Abraham defeated King Kedorlaomer and his allies in order to retrieve his nephew Lot, a prisoner of war. After his victory, Abraham traveled to Jerusalem, then known as Salem, where, moved by gratitude to God, he gave the priest Melchizedek ten percent of the spoils of that war. Centuries before Moses litigated a tithe, Abraham illustrated how the beloved of God respond to His grace with gratitude.

Abraham's experience has been replicated in countless lives throughout the history of the Church. Touched by the Spirit, God's beloved children, moved by grateful hearts, express their love for God by offering Him financial and material gifts. While we may offer such gifts at any time, Scripture illustrates that the regular gatherings of God's people typically include opportunities for such actions. Without a doubt, material or financial sacrifices characterized the worship of the Old Testament, and the New Testament church will not allow us to conclude that the perfect sacrifice of Christ relieves Christians of that practice.

In fact, in I Corinthians 16:2, we read, "On the first day of every week (planned), each one of you (personal) should set aside a sum of money in keeping with his income" (proportionate).

So, following the example of the Old Testament, we consider financial or material gifts as an act of worship, and following the example of Corinth, we practice personal, planned and proportionate giving. Our gifts, however, reflect a more encompassing gift. Following the example of the apostles and the teaching of Paul, we "offer our bodies to the Lord as living sacrifices, holy and pleasing to God – this is our spiritual act of worship" (Romans 12:1).

The Person Who Worships

We refer to this liturgical act as an "offering." That word implies "something freely given, something presented as a token of dedication or devotion." The purpose of the offering is "to give our first-fruits to God, to render to God a sacrifice of praise."[17] The meaning of the offering may be symbolized by an offertory procession, during which worshipers present their gifts to God with prayers and songs of gratitude and dedication.

The Bible offers specific direction for this liturgical act. First, we offer our gifts secretly. We don't announce how much we give (Matthew 6:1-4). Second, we practice joyful generosity for ""God loves a cheerful giver" (II Corinthians 9:5-6). In response to that mandate, some congregations applaud the announcement of the offering. In that the practice of clapping is associated with happiness, clapping for the offering engenders a spirit of cheer. Third, we give sacrificially. God desires more than the leftover scraps from our table. God gave his only Son who prescribes sacrificial giving, like that of the poor widow (Mark 12:41-43). Fourth, we give motivated by love. God loved and God gave. People drop money into the offering plate for a lot of reasons. Some give for tax advantages. Others give for the survival of their church. Some give out of a spirit of obligation. Some give to be seen. But unless love for God and neighbor motivates giving, it is not an act of worship.

In many churches deacons or other appointed persons collect the offerings and present them to God on behalf of the people. In others, worshipers leave their seats, step forward, and place their offerings in baskets at the front of the sanctuary. A prayer may be offered either before or after the offering, though it is perhaps most common to begin the offering with an announcement and invitation to give, and then to close the offering with a prayer of dedication.

The offering may include other forms of gifts, such as food, clothing, or supplies for a specific need. Congregations might keep a resource bank of members' abilities and spiritual gifts; periodic updates could take place during the offering. Musicians may offer their musical gifts while the rest of the congregation offers monetary gifts. Children may also offer musical gifts or receive the offering, or bring forward signs or symbols of their own gifts to God.

---

[17] *Worship Sourcebook* (Grand Rapids, MI: CRC Publications, 2004), 235-236.

Chapter Three
The People Who Worship

Principle #8 On the Gathering for Worship:
Worship requires people.

> *"Let us not give up meeting together, as some are in the habit of doing, but let us encourage one another – and all the more as you see the Day approaching." (Hebrews 10:25)*

Each Christian may worship the Lord privately while at work, rest or play. The exercise of corporate worship, however, requires that Christians leave their private lives to form an assembly with other Christians. The first movement of a liturgy, then, is the gathering of the people. By gathering we respond to God's invitation to worship Him. We receive this invitation through the written Word where we read, "Let us not give up meeting together." We also "hear" it through the inner working of the Holy Spirit who convinces us that we should "go to church." Prompted by the Spirit, we leave our homes, hop in our cars, and travel to our meeting place.

Few recognize "going to church" as a liturgical action, but when we leave our lives in this "present and concrete world, and drive fifteen miles or walk a few blocks, we establish the conditions for everything else that is to happen."[1] Our coming together, then, represents far more than commonly assumed. On the surface, it may seem like all we do is drag ourselves out of bed, put on some better-than-usual clothes, and rush off in our cars to "church." On a deeper level, however, when we leave our homes we are on our way "to constitute the Church," and when we arrive we are "transformed into the Church of God."[2] James F. White writes,

> There is an intentionality in... those who are called out from the world. It is so obvious that we usually forget it, but the most important thing that happens in Christian worship is that believers come together. Over the centuries, hundreds of thousands of Christians have been willing to die for the act of coming together in Christ's name. Their crime was not in what they did in worship but in making worship possible by assembling.[3]

The liturgical act of gathering together affirms a biblical understanding of the nature of the church. In over a hundred occasions in Scripture, the word "church" translates the Greek word, *ekklesia*, which, in the first century, was commonly used to refer "to an assembly of citizens called to decide matters of common welfare."[4] The first century church used the word *ekklesia* with reference to the actual gathering or concrete assembly of the believers. As the Catholic theologian Hans Küng notes, "there is no *ekklesia* in the intervals between them."[5]

But there is another layer of meaning. In the Greek translation of the Hebrew Old Testament, we discover that the word *ekklesia* translates the Hebrew word *qahal*, a designation for God's assembled people. At the foot of Mount Sinai, for example, Moses delivered the Ten Commandments to the *qahal*. We may conclude, then, that the church is not only a gathered

---

[1] Alexander Schmemann, *For the Life of the World: Sacraments and Orthodoxy*, (Crestwood, NY: St Vladimir's Seminary Press, 2002), 27.
[2] Alexander Schmemann, *For the Life of the World*, 27.
[3] James F. White, "How Do We Know It Is Us?," in *Liturgy and The Moral Self*, edited by E. Byron Anderson and Bruce T. Morrill (Collegeville, MN: The Liturgical Press, 1998), 64.
[4] Rodney Clapp, *A Peculiar People: The Church as culture in a post-Christian society* (Downers Grove, IL: InterVarsity Press, 1966), 80.
[5] Hans Küng, *The Church*, 118.

community, but one that belongs to the Lord. This conclusion receives additional support from the two occasions the New Testament uses *kyriakon* to refer to the Church. That Greek word refers to "that which belongs to the Lord" (I Corinthians 11:2 and Revelation 1:10).

When Jesus said "I will build my Church," then, he was not describing a generic gathering of people called together to vote on candidates in an election. Instead, he referred to the gathering of a people of God called out of darkness into light so that they may become a "chosen people, a royal priesthood, a holy nation, a people belonging to God" (I Peter 2:9). Such an understanding of the local church harmonizes with our traditional understanding of the one, holy, catholic and apostolic Church. As the Heidelberg Catechism teaches, Jesus, "through his Spirit and Word, out of the entire human race, from the beginning of the world to its end, gathers, protects, and preserves for himself, a community chosen for eternal life and united in true faith."[6] This community is a not an abstract theory, but a "real people of God in the world, a real spiritual society, a real body of Christ actually present in the world, a place where the light of God really shines and the life of God really pulses."[7]

This principle specifically influences how we gather for worship. As individuals arrive on the campus and approach the center for worship, opportunities arise to greet fellow worshipers. We verbally acknowledge each other's presence and exchange some form of affection. We shake hands with some, hug others, and "holy kiss" a few, unless your culture, like that of some of my Greek friends, encourages you to double holy kiss everyone you meet. The most natural place for the mutual greeting is not in the sanctuary, prompted by the liturgist or pastor. While such action is better than nothing, the best place for mutual greeting is where the congregants initially encounter one another. Congregants may greet one another in the parking lot, on the side walk, in the lobby or narthex of the sanctuary. Some congregations position "greeters" at those locations for that purpose. Others encourage fellowship between seated congregants waiting for the worship service to begin. Still others choose to reserve the sanctuary for silent meditation and preparation for worship while, at the same time, encouraging social interaction between congregants in a space outside the

---

[6]The Heidelberg Catechism Lord's Day 21, Answer 54.
[7]Leslie Newbigin, *The Household of God*, 53.

sanctuary. On that point, it seems best that congregations choose one or the other and then make that choice known to all. Personally, I promote social interaction between gathering congregants anywhere from the parking lot to the pew. I find it to be an excellent way for brothers and sisters in Christ to prepare for corporate worship.

The social interaction between friends in Christ will naturally include expressions of love, such as "laughter, applause, delight, and enthusiasm."[8] Consequently, there will be an atmosphere of "festival." The space where the saints gather will be filled the noise of people greeting one another, rejoicing with one another, mourning with one another. They will call one another by name before they, together, call upon the Name which is above all names.

Of course, the greetings of those gathering for worship can be reduced to nothing more than an exchange of meaningless pleasantries. It can be reduced to nods and gestures, to "Good Morning" and "Beautiful Day." It can replicate the mutual greetings at the work place or in school. As Christians, however, the mutual greeting, in a liturgical setting, may affirm our identity as royal priesthood and a people belonging to God. As brothers and sisters in Christ, why limit a greeting to "Good Morning," when we can say so much more? After a long week on the spiritual battlefield as soldiers of Christ, should we not greet one another with "Shalom" or "Grace be to you" or "Praise the Lord" or "The Lord be with you"? Why talk about the weather when we can affirm our status as people created by God the Father, redeemed by Jesus Christ, and indwelt by the Holy Spirit?

Principle #9 On the Unity of the Worshipers: We worship as one.

"I pray for those who will believe in me through their message, that all of them may be one." (John 17:20-21)

---

[8] Howard L. Rice & James C. Huffstutler, *Reformed Worship* (Louisville, KY: Geneva Press, 2001), 195.

Principled Worship

I once worshiped with a self-described "seeker-sensitive" Protestant congregation. This congregation had adopted a philosophy of allowing guests to visit anonymously. So, I entered the lobby and found a seat near the front of the sanctuary without receiving a greeting from anyone. Several minutes later, a young, professional-looking man sat down next to me. I looked at him as he seated himself, hoping to greet him, exchange names, and, perhaps, even shake hands. However, he failed to look my way. In response, I kept looking at him, hoping he might signal an opening to which I might respond with a greeting in the name of Jesus. But he only looked away. His behavior led me conclude that he must be a "seeker." After all, how could a brother in Christ sit in worship and not greet the brother in Christ sitting beside him? Based on my assumption, I decided I better give him "space." But a little later into the liturgy, this same man was standing beside me, with his arms raised to heaven, singing praises to God. I turned to him again, waiting for any kind greeting, but it never came.

How did that happen? Clearly, the person sitting beside me believed that corporate worship provides individuals with opportunities for individual encounters with God. From my perspective, he viewed the church as a collection of disconnected individuals. He found it acceptable to express love for God, while ignoring the person sitting next to him. That experience convicted me of the need to affirm the obvious: corporate worship is corporate.

When we gather, we do so as one people, not a collection of individuals. We, as a gathered community, are a single body of Christ (Ephesians 1:22-23), enjoying a sevenfold unity described by the apostle Paul: "one body, united by one Spirit, called to one hope, in one Lord, to one faith and one baptism in Jesus Christ, created and called by one God who is over all and through all and in all" (Ephesians 4:4-6). We may conclude, then, that even if a congregation includes two-year olds and eighty-two year olds, truck drivers and professors, Dutch and Italian immigrants, it is one body. God graces the gathered community with a unity that comes from outside of itself and in spite of itself.

By identifying worship as a corporate activity, we suppress our desire to approach it as individual consumers seeking self-fulfillment. Of course, once in a while, and more often than we may admit, we attend a worship service without concern for the gathered community. We go to "get something out of it." So, we walk from the parking lot, offer a few verbal pleasantries to people on our path, fill space in the sanctuary, offer personal prayers and praise to God, hear a sermon, leave the presence of the gathered community, and return to our lives. In other words, we pretty much ignore the people while seeking nourishment for our own souls. Unfortunately, when we approach worship as a solitary experience, we miss out on the unique grace of God made available through the Body of Christ, a temple of the Holy Spirit. We also fail to strengthen and celebrate our fellowship with one another.

When we come to worship for self-fulfillment, we expect a liturgy that "meets our needs." If it doesn't, we may try to change the worship service by filing our complaints with those responsible for planning the liturgy. Complaining differs from concerns that flow from love for God or love for others. Complaining flows from a selfish heart. Those who complain expect every aspect of the liturgy to match their preferences. In my lifetime, I have witnessed countless congregations fail to distinguish between concerns and complaints. They have granted equal weight to concerns prompted by love and complaints prompted by selfishness, i.e., sin. They have, in other words, equated biblical principles with preferences. Those with the awesome responsibility of planning and overseeing corporate worship hold the tremendous responsibility of distinguishing between the two so that their liturgies are shaped, not by preferences, but by the Word and Spirit of God.

Our identity as one body influences our approach to corporate worship. Since we belong to Christ and His Church, we understand that, even in worship, we should make "every effort to keep the unity of the Spirit (Ephesians 4:3). In the "Sermon on the Mount, for example, Jesus taught us to repair fractured relationships with fellow Christians before we worship with them. In Matthew 5:23-24 we read,

> If you are offering your gift at the altar and there remember that your brother has something against you, leave your gift there in front of the altar. First go and be reconciled to your brother; then offer your gift.

Traditionally, Reformed Christians have insisted on such preparation before reception of the Sacrament of the Lord's Supper. My denominationally-approved form, read before participation in the Lord's Supper, reads, "Since

Christ, by his death, resurrection and ascension has obtained for us the life-giving Spirit who unites us all in one body, we should receive the Lord's Supper in brotherly love, mindful of the communion of saints."[9]

My father has taken those words seriously. Several years ago he had a heart attack, followed with by-pass surgery. While in the hospital, he did not receive a visit from his pastor, but he didn't expect one since the pastor was on vacation. However, my father learned that the pastor visited another hospitalized parishioner during the same time he was in the hospital. This angered him and didn't help his recovery. He held on to the anger for a few weeks, but then faced a dilemma. The Lord's Supper would be served the coming Sunday, and he believed he should not participate in the Lord's Supper until he reconciled with the pastor. So my father, a man of few words, drove to the pastor's home on a Saturday morning to initiate a conversion that led to reconciliation with his pastor. My dad understood what we must all grasp: worship is not a private affair. One cannot love God without, at the same time, loving one's neighbor.

Principle #10 On the Covenant of the Worshipers: We Worship Within a Covenanted Community

"Therefore, as we have opportunity, let us do good to all people, especially to those who belong to the family of believers." (Galatians 6:10)

The triune God, who has lived in eternal fellowship as Father, Son and Holy Spirit, has blessed Christians with the gift of community. He has allowed us a taste of heaven here on earth. Our fellowship, then, is not something we create through membership or other means. It transcends the depth of our fellowship with family or friends. It supercedes the fellowship we may have had as immigrants speaking a common language. Christian fellowship flows from the eternal fellowship enjoyed by our Triune God. Plus, it transforms strangers into brothers and sisters. It breaks down walls and includes people of all nations. It creates unity with vibrant diversity.

---

[9]"The Order for the Sacrament of the Lord's Supper," in *The Liturgy of the Reformed Church in America* (New York: Board of Education, 1968), 64.

The People Who Worship

The First Church in Jerusalem illustrates this principle. In Acts 2 we discover a vibrant, dynamic and unified fellowship characterized by the study of God's Word, sacrificial stewardship, generosity, and worship. Dr. Gilbert Bilezekian, as told by Bill Hybels, summarizes that unique and amazing event in this way:

> There was once a community of believers... so totally devoted to God that their life together was charged with the Spirit's power. In that band of Christ-followers, believers loved each other with a radical kind of love. They took off their masks and shared their lives together. They laughed and cried and prayed and sang and served together in authentic Christian fellowship. Those who had more shared freely with those who had less until socio-economic barriers melted away. People related together in ways that bridged gender and racial chasms, and celebrated cultural differences. Acts 2 tells us that this community of believers, this church, offered unbelievers a vision of life that was so beautiful it took their breath away. It was so bold, so creative, so dynamic that they couldn't resist it.[10]

"People who belong to such a community," writes Rodney Clapp, "want to belong to it. They cannot imagine worthwhile life without it."[11]

But that may not be your experience of church. The reason? Sin has subverted the gift of community in many congregations. Sin broke the fellowship of Adam and Eve with God and their fellowship with one another. Years later, sin entered the heart of Cain who murdered his brother. Some time later, sin entered the hearts of those who constructed a tower of Babel, not for the sake of community, but for themselves. Since that time, sin has subverted the fellowship of countless congregations. Unfortunately, one may look over the history of the Christian Church and conclude that few congregations treasure the gift of community, recognize the threat to community, confess their failures in maintaining community, and, then, experience the fellowship of the Triune God.

The apostle Paul offers plenty of advice for congregations seeking to enjoy unity with diversity. In a series of mandates, each of which includes

---

[10] Bill Hybels, *Courageous Leadership* (Grand Rapids, MI: Zondervan, 2002), 17-18.
[11] Rodney Clapp, *A Peculiar People*, 187-211.

the phrase "One another," he tells us how to live as communities of believers:

> Romans 12:10 - Honor one another above yourselves.
> Romans 12:16 - Live in harmony with one another.
> Romans 14:12 - Don't pass judgment on one another.
> Romans 15:7 - Accept one another as Christ has accepted you.
> Romans 15:14 - Instruct one another.
> Romans 16:16 - Greet one another with a holy kiss.
> I Corinthians 1:10 - Agree with one another.
> Galatians 5:13 - Serve one another in love.
> Ephesians 4:2 - Bear with one another in love.
> Ephesians 4:32 - Be kind and compassionate to one another.
> Ephesians 5:19 - Speak to one another with psalms, hymns, and spiritual songs.
> Ephesians 5:21 - Submit to one another.
> Colossians 3:16 - Admonish one another.
> I Thessalonians 5:11 - Encourage one another.

Those mandates provide the skeleton of the covenant that should exist between fellow Christians within a local congregation. Some congregations, however, have found it helpful to develop even more specific covenants. The members of the Crossroads Church in Madison, Wisconsin, for example, promise to "protect the unity of the church, share the responsibility of the church, and serve the ministry of the church." Members of congregations within the Reformed Church in America have each promised:

> To make faithful use of the means of grace, especially the hearing of the Word and the use of the Sacraments; to give faithful adherence to the doctrines and teaching of the Church; to walk in the spirit of Christian fellowship and love with the congregation; to offer faithfully to the service of God your prayers and gifts; and to seek the things that make for purity and peace in the Church of Jesus Christ as long as you live.[12]

---

[12] "The Order for Admission to the Lord's Table of Those Baptized in Infancy," in *The Liturgy of the Reformed Church in America* (New York: Board of Education, 1968), 57.

Congregational covenants like those shape our expectations of one another. They may even lead to the practice of church discipline. In I Corinthians 5, for example, the apostle Paul encourages the Corinthian Church to "expel the wicked men" from among them (5:13). In the next chapter, the apostle Paul shames the Corinthian Church by encouraging them to settle their legal disputes "in house," rather than in civil courts (6:5). His insistence on church discipline and the acknowledgement of disputes among believers in Christ affirms the implicit covenant that exists between brothers and sisters in Christ who enjoy the fellowship of the Triune God. Following the teaching of Jesus, Paul expects local congregations to reflect the unity of the Godhead.

In summary, we may assume that "members" of any Christian congregation or church family have promised to love one another in such a way that the ministry and mission of the congregation flourishes. We would hope that Christians long to model the First Church in Jerusalem whose community life attracted unbelievers. We may pray that brothers and sisters in Christ would live in loving unity so that the world may observe and glorify God (John 17:21), that they would distinguish themselves as an authentic Christian community.[13] The good news? In such a caring community, inter-dependence will create wholistic environments, people of all capacities and fallibilities will be incorporated, creativity will be multiplied rather than channeled, and individualized responses will be normative.[14]

Our covenant relationship as a community tangibly influences liturgical life in several ways. First, a membership covenant often creates a multi-generational congregation which, in turn, requires a liturgy that allows multiple generations to worship with one heart and one voice. That's a tough challenge, prompting some to give up and offer generational-specific liturgies. But it is not impossible. Congregations that have designed multi-generational liturgies have not only bore witness to their unity in Christ but, in the process, have discovered that children enjoy worshiping with their grandparents, and that retired folk enjoy fellowship with teens.[15]

---

[13] Rodney Clapp, *A Peculiar People*, 187-211.
[14] John McKnight, *The Careless Society* (New York: BasicBooks, 1995), 167.
[15] See Gil Rendle, *The Multigenerational Congregation* (Bethseda, MD: The Alban Institute, 2002).

Second, our covenant relationship encourages the development of liturgies that sustain and enrich authentic Christian community. We may hope that our weekly gathering opens avenues for the sharing of life and faith, thanksgiving and lamentation, as well as opportunities for vulnerability before our brothers and sisters in Christ. Herein lies the power of the "Prayers for the People" and personal testimonies. Through the sharing of our concerns and our struggles, we express and build our community as brothers and sisters in Christ.[16]

Herein also lies the rational for including announcements within the liturgy. Through them we share housekeeping matters peculiar to our church life, such as the time, place, and date for a particular gathering or ministry. We also "rejoice with those who rejoice and mourn with those who mourn" (Romans 12:15) by verbally highlighting joys and concerns. In that same spirit, we may acknowledge, even applaud momentous events in the lives of individual members, such as the baptism of a child or the 50th anniversary of a couple. We may update our prayer lists with the names of those who have lost health or love or life. So, while announcements are not an act of worship, they hold an important place in the liturgy as a means of building authentic community.

Principle #11 On the Seekers in Worship:
The visible congregation differs from the invisible.

Many will say to me on that day, "Lord, Lord, did we not prophesy in your name, and in your name drive out demons and perform many miracles. Then I will say to them plainly, "I never knew you. Away from me, you evildoers." (Matthew 7:22-23)

The gathered assembly is a mixed community. It includes both believers and unbelievers. We have traditionally articulated that conviction by referring to the gathered people as the "visible" church, and by referring to the elect, those who have or will come to saving faith in Jesus Christ, as the "invisible church." That distinction accents the sovereign work of

---

[16]For the link between fellowship and liturgy see Elsie Ann McKee, "Reformed Worship in the Sixteenth Century," in *Christian Worship in Reformed Churches Past and Present*, 23-24.

The People Who Worship

God in salvation but also reminds us that the worshipping community, more often than not, includes three types of people: the elect who have come to saving faith, pretenders or professors who are not elect, and the elect who have not yet, but will, come to faith.

The elect who have come to saving faith attend corporate worship as forgiven sinners. While we don't always admit it, we come weary in need of rest, weak in need of strength, and broken in need of healing. Our Sunday suits and hats may suggest otherwise, but we know the truth: we are sinning saints. So, as the outstanding New Testament scholar N.T. Wright writes,

> We come into the presence of Almighty God, to feast at his table, not because we are good people, but because we are forgiven sinners. We come, as we come to a doctor, not because we are all well but because we are all sick. We come, not because we've got it all together, but because God's got it all together and has invited us to join him. We come, not because our hands are full of our own self-importance or self-righteousness, but because they are empty and waiting to receive his love, his body and blood, his own very self.[17]

The pretenders, or non-elect professors, constitute another group of worshipers. Jesus identifies this group during his "Sermon on the Mount." It includes religious people, perhaps raised in the church, who may accurately be described as "going through the motions." For them Christianity serves purposes other than redemption. They come to worship for any number of reasons except for one: to worship the Lord.

We, the elect, find it difficult to distinguish pretenders from us for, in many ways, they look just like us. But that is not our responsibility. When it comes to such matters, the Lord teaches us not to pass judgment (Matthew 7:1-2). Yet, we should never forget that one or more among us may be pretenders just faking it. Such an acknowledgement, however, should also prompt self-examination. It should encourage the elect to assure themselves that they are not just going through the motions.

Traditionally, pastors and theologians have labeled the third group of worshipers as "awakened sinners." This group includes the elect who have

---

[17] N.T. Wright, *For All God's Worth*, 79-80.

not yet come to faith in Jesus Christ. While they have not yet professed faith in Christ, the Spirit has begun his gracious work within them. We may even say that they have been born again for they, unlike those who have no place for God (Romans 3:10-18), experience the working of the Spirit in their souls. Consequently, as the liturgy unfolds, they are drawn in. When the Word is preached, they hear God speaking directly to them.

John Nevin is one of many writers who has encouraged pastors and congregations to assume the presence of awakened sinners in every service:

> It should be taken for granted that there are always such persons in his congregation, and he should not think that they are to be found only during commotions. Wherever the Gospel is preached faithfully, there is always an inquiring party, especially among the young, holding a middle position between the obedient and the callous. They should be regarded as a standing class.[18]

How does the constituency of the gathered community influence the liturgy? How does the presence of three different types of people in one gathered community shape the worship of that people? First, it creates optimism. We plan worship with hope that the Word of the Lord will be heard and received by believers, as well as unbelievers. With John Nevin, we assume that a person, awakened by the Holy Spirit, will hear anew the Gospel and apply it to his heart. Many congregations, especially those in mainline traditions, hesitate or refuse to verbalize hope for awakened sinners to come to saving faith during the weekly liturgy. Still more don't have a clear process or procedure by which an awakened sinner might take such a step. Ask yourself this question, "If, last Sunday, an awakened sinner was convicted by the preaching of the Gospel, does that person know what to do with that feeling?" Has the congregation provided an opportunity for adults to ask, like the Philippian jailer, "What must I do to be saved?"

Second, it creates multiple responses to liturgical renewal. During my tenure as pastor of the Palos Heights Christian Reformed Church,

---

[18] John W. Nevin, *The Reformed Pastor: Lectures on Pastoral Theology*, edited by Sam Hamstra, Jr. (Eugene, Oregon: Wipf & Stock Publishers, 2006), 76-77.

the Elders and I have received many responses to liturgical change and development. As expected, most of the people go with the flow, dutifully following the lead of the Elders. Yet God has blessed us with believers who ask questions. When, for example, the liturgy did not include a "Prayer of Confession," I was asked how I could claim that the liturgy was Reformed. That question, and many more like it, has proved invaluable to our liturgical life as a congregation. But the congregation also includes pretenders who occasionally show their true colors by rejecting any attempts at liturgical renewal. My point is that such responses shouldn't surprise those responsible for planning worship. After all, why would the spiritual dead want a living liturgy?

Principle #12 On the Identity of the Worshipers: We worship as the body of Christ.

> *"Now you are the body of Christ, and each one of you is a part of it." (I Corinthians 12:27)*

The Palos Heights Christian Reformed Church baptizes the infant children of its professing members. During the sacrament, the parent or parents acknowledge God's grace, their child's guilt, and their gratitude to God by responding positively to these questions:

> First, do you confess Jesus Christ as your Lord and Savior, accept the promises of God, and affirm the truth of the Christian faith which is proclaimed in the Bible and confessed in this church of Christ?
>
> Second, do you believe that your child, though sinful by nature, is received by God in Christ as a member of his covenant, and therefore ought to be baptized?
>
> Third, do you promise, in reliance on the Holy Spirit and with the help of the Christian community, to do all in your power to instruct your child in the Christian faith and to lead him/her by your example to be Christ's disciples?

Having heard the promise of parents to raise their child in the way of the Lord, with the help of the Church, the congregation answers this question:

> Do you, the people of the Lord, promise to receive this child in love, pray for him or her, help instruct him or her in the faith, and encourage and sustain him or her in the fellowship of believers?

That's a huge promise for parents as well as for members of the congregation. It calls congregants to more than serving as a nursery attendant or Sunday school teacher. It requires a congregation with the heart, mind, and hands of Christ. It calls professing members to practice unconditional love for each of the children in the congregation with the hope that, with God's help, no child will ever stray from the person of Christ because of the Church of Christ. It reminds believers that the local church is the only Christ baptized young children will see until they gain the ability to understand the powerful stories about Jesus in the Bible.

Our identity as the body of Christ not only influences how we relate to children, but also shapes our relationships with guests. We open our liturgies to any stranger who walks through the doors and takes his or her place in the gathering space. We have a church sign just off the road upon which we post our service times and even put a big "Welcome." We provide worship tools that enable each person to participate in the liturgy.

In addition and more importantly, when guests arrive, we, the body of Christ, have an opportunity to reflect the character, compassion and love of Christ. In other words, we may exercise the biblical gift of hospitality, which may be defined as our "response of love and gratitude for God's love and welcome to us."[19] Hospitality is not an option for the body of Christ. It is, as Nouwen writes, "obligatory for Christians to offer an open and hospitable space where strangers can cast off their strangeness and become our fellow human beings."[20] But the motive for hospitality surpasses obligation; it also includes expectation. When we gather with

---

[19] Christine Pohl, *Making Room: Recovering Hospitality as a Christian Tradition* (Grand Rapids, MI: Eerdmans Publishing Co, 1999), 172.

[20] Henri Nouwen, *Reaching Out* (New York: Doubleday & Company, Inc., 1975), 46, 54.

our guests we become a unique combination of people, one that may include angels (Hebrews 13:2) and Jesus Christ himself (Matthew 18:6). It was Saint Benedict who adopted this rule: "Let all guests who arrive be received like Christ for He is going to say, 'I came as a guest and you received me.'"[21]

Many congregations confused hospitality with friendliness. Friendly congregations do a good job of greeting people as they arrive on campus and enter the sanctuary. They have a visitor-friendly liturgy that includes a personal welcome and both verbal and written directives that allow for their maximum participation. But, truth be told, friendly congregations extend friendliness to encourage guests to join and become like them. Hospitality moves beyond friendliness. It not only greets people but welcomes and enfolds them on their terms. Thomas Long writes:

> To be sure, people need to be treated with kindness and generosity. They need to be welcomed into the house and graciously invited to the table, but that is not all they need…. Viewed theologically, people need to be welcomed into God's house, recognized and known by name, and joined with others in offering their lives to God in acts of mission.[22]

No modern writer has captured the heart of hospitality with greater passion and precision than the late-Dutch pastor-theologian, Henri Nouwen. In "Wounded Healer," he defines hospitality as the "ability to pay attention to the guest." He, then, offers this description:

> Hospitality is the virtue which allows us to break through the narrowness of our own fears and to open our houses to the stranger, with the intuition that salvation comes to us in the form of a tired traveler. Hospitality makes anxious disciples into powerful witnesses, makes suspicious owners into generous givers, and makes close-minded sectarians into interested recipients of new ideas and insights.[23]

---

[21] *The Rule of Saint Benedict,* Chapter 53: "The Reception of Guests."
[22] Thomas C. Long, *Beyond the Worship Wars,* 35.
[23] Henri Nouwen, *The Wounded Healer* (New York: Doubleday, 1972), 89.

Principled Worship

In *Reaching Out,* Nouwen offers this complimentary description of hospitality, with its obvious application to our weekly gatherings:

> Hospitality is not to change people, but to offer them space where change can take place. It is not to bring men and women over to our side, but to offer freedom not disturbed by dividing lines. It is not to lead our neighbor into a corner where there are no alternatives left, but to open a wide spectrum of options for choice and commitment. It is not an educated intimidation with good books, good stories and good works, but the liberation of fearful hearts so that words can find roots and bear ample fruit. It is not a method of making our God and our way into the criteria of happiness, but the opening of an opportunity to others to find their God and their way.[24]

Why do so many congregations struggle with hospitality? Some have concluded that too many congregations have become inwardly focused and need to become externally focused.[25] There is some truth to that. As Nouwen wrote, hospitality is very difficult when we are "preoccupied with our own needs, worries, and tension, which prevent us from taking distance from ourselves in order to pay attention to others."[26] But I am not comfortable with an either-or proposition which, in the end, often forces congregants to choose between hospitality to guests and ministry to their children. Worshipers must be Christ to both. Hence, the solution cannot come by neglecting one and prioritizing another.

The key to hospitality is to correct our preoccupation with ourselves with constant reminders that Christ is present with us both in the "body of Christ" and in the guest. On one hand, we are the body of Christ. In our relationships as fellow church members, we must create "free and fearless space where brotherhood and sisterhood can be formed and fully experienced.... to offer space where people are encouraged to disarm themselves, to lay aside their occupations and preoccupations, and to listen with attention and care to the voice speaking in their own center."[27] On

---

[24] Henri Nouwen, *Reaching Out*, 51.
[25] For example, Rick Rusaw and Eric Swanson, *The Externally Focused Church* (Loveland, CO: Group Publishing, 2004).
[26] Henri Nouwen, *The Wounded Healer*, 89.
[27] Henri Nouwen, *Reaching Out*, 46, 54.

the other hand, each time we open the doors to the gathering space, we hope for the opportunity to welcome guests into our fellowship, realizing that, in so doing, we may welcome Christ.

Congregations seeking to create a culture of hospitality may take a few practical steps. First, they may identify those within their memberships with excellent social or people skills to serve as official hosts for worship. They may select individuals to greet in the parking lot, open doors, greet inside the doors, and the like. Unfortunately, some congregations, while they do not expect every member to sing in the choir, expect every member to greet guests. That's a recipe for trouble. Not every one can handle that simple task in a way that benefits both the church and the guest.

Second, liturgists may offer a verbal welcome to guests and, during the "Prayers for the People," pray specifically for the guests. Those practices sensitize the congregation to the presence of guests. Over time, they help develop a congregational culture of concern for those God has led into their presence.

Third, those responsible for hospitality may visit other congregations and learn – good or bad – from them. They may also ask people from other congregations or from the community to visit them. My wife, Debbie, has been a "Mystery Shopper." She was paid to visit retail stores, purchase products, return them, and, then, write a detailed review of her experience. Congregations might ask some individuals who have never worshiped with them, to visit, worship, and report on their experience. They might discover that their signage, for example, is woefully inadequate, or that the facility, in one way or another, discourages people from entering.

Fourth, those responsible for creating and sustaining a culture of hospitality may learn a few things from those in the business world whose livelihood depends on the greeting of guests. The Applebee's Restaurant, for example, advertises itself as a "neighborhood restaurant." Interestingly, when I go there, the host or hostess opens the door for me and offers a verbal greeting. I discover a similar practice at the local Blockbuster store. Each time I experience those greetings I first wonder how my congregation measures up, hoping that we, the body of Christ, filled with the Spirit, reflect the kindness of the Lord to each guest who visits us.

Fifth, congregations may find it helpful to identify those who are not welcome. While that may sound harsh, the exercise simply helps a congregation identify potential areas for change. Some worship centers, for example, prohibit access by individuals in wheelchairs. Most liturgies prohibit participation by individuals with one or more impairments: cognitive, visual, sight, or sound. Every congregation, by choosing a worship tongue, hinders participation by several people groups. When a congregation determines the context for its weekly gathering, it naturally excludes some from gathering.

Principle #13 On the Leaders of Worship: God equips individuals to lead worship.

> *"But to each one of us grace has been given as Christ apportioned it." (Ephesians 4:7)*

Why do we have postal service? In part, we have postal service because people enjoy expressing their love for others through letters, cards, and gifts. The desire of one person to communicate with another, then, creates the need for someone with the responsibility to deliver the communiqué in a timely and courteous manner. The answer: the postal worker.

Why do we have designated worship leaders? The God who has called us to worship has a Word for a people who also have a word for God. By the very act of gathering, then, the congregation creates responsibilities and opportunities. Who will facilitate the dialogue between God and His people? Who will deliver the Word from God? Who prompts the praise and prayers of the people to God? The biblical and theological answer: those gifted and called by God for such service.

The first half of that twofold prerequisite is giftedness. Scripture teaches us that the God who calls His people to worship equips His people for worship. The Holy Spirit, in particular, gifts individuals within the congregation for liturgical service to the congregation. We find this assurance in at least three passages. In his first letter to the Corinthians, the apostle Paul writes,

> There are different kinds of gifts, but the same Spirit. There are different kinds of service, but the same Lord. There are different kinds of working, but the same God works all of them in all men. Now to each one the manifestation of the Spirit is given for the common good (12:4-7).

In Romans 12:6 Paul writes that "we have different gifts, according to the grace given us." He echoes that promise in his letter to the Ephesians: "But to each one of us grace has been given as Christ apportioned it" (4:7).

Interestingly, most of the gifts mentioned by the apostle Paul may be classified as "liturgical," or as having their primary place of service within the worship of God's people. Those responsible for supervising worship, then, may confidently survey the congregation within which they will discover individuals gifted by God for the responsibility of leading part or all of a worship service.

In fact, the giftedness of the particular individuals within a congregation, or brought into a congregation, will shape, in some degree, the corporate worship of a local congregation. One congregation, for example, may have gifted individuals able to communicate with the hearing-impaired. Another congregation may include gifted musicians who form an ensemble that accompanies congregational singing. Still another will have non-ordained individuals equipped to preach while the resident pastor is on vacation. Each congregation has a unique DNA of spiritual gifts that translate into a unique hour or more of worship.

The second half of the prerequisite for liturgical service is a call from God and His church. Individuals invested with the responsibility of leading worship should receive a two-fold call: the internal call from God and the external call from the church. The internal call comes mysteriously through the work of the Holy Spirit, who not only gifts believers but urges them to use their gifts in the service of the church. The Holy Spirit nudges gifted believers to consider accepting the huge responsibility of engaging the community of faith in the highest activity on earth.

Faithful followers of Christ need the inner call of the Holy Spirit for they constantly lament their personal weaknesses while lifting up the grandeur of worship. The comparison between the two suppresses any desire to thrust self forward for liturgical service. It creates doubt which suppresses faith in God's giftedness, encouraging them to sit in the bleachers, where it is safe, rather than walk on the court. But God doesn't relent. The Holy Spirit keeps prodding the gifted to faithfully acknowledge their gifts and lovingly use them.

The external call of the church plays an equally important role. It protects the church from those who throw themselves forward as God's answer to the congregation's need. It compensates for pride which, left alone, pushes believers forward when they don't have the appropriate gifts for the positions their sinful hearts desire. Most importantly, the external call of the church compliments the internal call already at work within the heart of believers. The call of the church, then, offers a process by which a congregation may identify and affirm gifted individuals for service in its worship ministry.

The call of the Church comes from the person or group of persons ultimately responsible for worship. In other words, it comes from those who hold and exercise the authority of Christ, the Head of the church. Episcopalians believe that Christ has invested the bishop with His authority; Presbyterians believe that Christ has invested the elders with His authority; Congregationalists believe that Christ has invested the congregation with His authority.

The Christian Reformed Church, of which I am a part, believes that Christ has delegated his authority to the Council, a body that includes elders and deacons. The Council, according to our church order, delegates the authority to supervise worship to the Elders who, in turn, grant me, the pastor, the privilege of planning and leading worship. They supervise me in this task, approving every initiative for our multi-generational worship services. All of that to say that I have been called by God through the Council to lead worship for the Palos Heights Christian Reformed Church.

Who should lead worship? Those Christians who believe they have been gifted by God for such service and those whom God has called to such a responsibility. For some congregations, this group of believers receives ordination. This rite, practiced throughout the centuries, minimally denotes installation into a position of responsibility, accompanied by the laying of hands upon the candidate.[28] Traditionally, ordination has been limited to Ministers of the Word and Sacraments, i.e., pastors, and the leadership of worship has been limited to the ordained. The Lutheran *Larger Catechism*, for example, limits the public reading of Scripture to the ordained. Many Reformed Christians, as another example, believe that only the ordained pastor may officiate public worship.

---

[28] For an outstanding study of this rite, see Marjorie Warkentin's *Ordination: A Biblical-Historical View* (Grand Rapids, MI: Eerdmans Publishing Co., 1982).

The People Who Worship

My experience suggests that the church gravely errs when it limits the responsibility of leading worship to those ordained as Ministers of the Word. First, those gifted as preachers may or may not be gifted as worship leaders or liturgists. Second, those not licensed through ordination may be gifted to lead worship in one capacity or another. If we are to be faithful to the Pauline teaching of spiritual gifts, it may be time for some to revisit the practice of limiting the leadership role in worship to ordained Ministers of the Word. Todd Nichol and Marc Kolden, for example, speaking as Lutherans, encourage us to "create and reform or abandon any other offices than the proper service of the Word and the world requires."[29]

Perhaps the best framework for discussing the leadership of worship is not ordination, but vocation, a term that derives from a Latin word that means "I call." Many Christians, especially those of Reformed ilk, use the term "vocation" to describe God's call upon individual believers to participate in His sovereign care of creation and the church. Of course, God doesn't need us to care for His creation or His church. When it comes to the worship, if He so desired, God could lead every part of the liturgy. But He has determined to care for creation and for His church through those gifted and called to such service. Towards that goal, God calls some to be pastors and other teachers, some to be plumbers and others electricians, some to be husbands and others wives, some to be parents and others children, some to be corporate executives and others homemakers, some to be truck drivers and others mechanics, some to be students and others teachers, some to be laborers and others pray-ers. God calls each believer to particular tasks, jobs, positions, or roles in life. In the end, each Christian may hold a handful of vocations at the same time. He even calls and equips some, with or without ordination and graduate school training, to lead particular liturgical acts.

In order that we may fulfill the responsibilities which accompany our vocations, we pray to God for both faith and love. We need faith so that we may believe, without doubt, that the God who has called us will equip us. It is so easy to find fault with ourselves, to back out of opportunities for service, to allow someone else to fill our role. So, we pray for faith sufficient to say with Paul, "I can do all things through Christ who strengthens me"

---

[29] Todd Nichol and Marc Kolden, editors, *Called and Ordained: Lutheran Perspectives on the Office of the Ministry* (Minneapolis, MN: Fortress Press, 1990), 224.

(Philippians 4:13). And, since we don't want to be nothing more than a noisy gong, we pray for love to accompany our service. We know that, in the end, vocation is all about love for neighbor. Gustaf Wingren writes,

> Vocation belongs to this world, not to heaven. It is directed toward one's neighbor not toward God. In his vocation one is not teaching up to God, but rather bends oneself down toward the world. When one does that, God's creative work is carried on. God's work of love takes form on earth, and that which is external witnesses to God's love.[30]

Faith and love do not negate the need for the called to prepare themselves for service by developing their God-given gifts. Through casual observation, we learn that divine gifts, like a garden, benefit from cultivation and maturation. It is possible but not probable that craftsmen, like Bezalel of Uri, wake up one morning with abilities they didn't have the day before simply because the Lord filled him with the "Spirit of God, with skill, ability and knowledge in all kinds of crafts" (Exodus 35:31). More often, the gifted prepare themselves for service, even as the apostles were prepared by our Lord. Minimally, they study the theological framework within which they exercise their gifts, as well as the particulars of the craft to which they have been called. Herein lies one excellent reason for seminary training.

I suggest, then, that the best foundation upon which to identify and call individuals to the awesome responsibility of leading one or more parts of worship is vocation. Let the church encourage its members to consider if the Spirit of God has gifted them for liturgical service. Let the church encourage the gifted to hone their craft through theological and practical training. Let the church call and install those gifted and called by the Spirit to assume places of responsibility for worship.

---

[30] Gustaf Wingren, *Luther On Vocation*, translated by Carl C. Rasmussen (Evansville, IN: Ballast Press, 1999), 10.

Chapter Four
The Content of Worship

Principle #14 On the Sermon in Worship:
We hope to receive a Word from the Lord.

> *"And we also thank God continually because, when you received the word of God, which you heard from us, you accepted it not as the word of men, but as it actually is, the word of God, which is at work in you who believe." (I Thessalonians 4:15)*

Throughout the history of redemption, God speaks and we listen. He initiates and we believe. He commands and we obey. We find that same pattern in worship: God calls and we respond. The liturgy, then, provides the framework for a conversation between heaven and earth, between God and the corporate assembly of saints. Some refer to this as the dialogical principle of worship.[1]

During the liturgy, we speak individually to the Lord through both audible and silent words. We also speak to the Lord corporately through songs and prayers of praise, thanksgiving, confession, intercession and

---

[1] D.G. Hart and John R. Muether, *With Reverence and Awe: Returning to the Basics of Reformed Worship* (Phillipsburg, NJ: P&R Publishing, 2002), 107.

petition. As recipients of God's grace, our hearts overflow with adoration and gratitude. Convicted by his holiness and our shortcomings, we humbly confess our sins, seeking assurance of forgiveness. Moved by love for neighbor and by a desire to obey God's word, we offer prayers for others, even our enemies. Finally, we humbly and confidently approach the throne of grace, seeking a word from the Lord.

God speaks to us through several voices, each made possible by the Holy Spirit. He speaks to us first and foremost through Christ the Incarnate Word, the Word of Life. He speaks to us through the Scriptures, the revealed or Written Word of God. He speaks to us through the sacraments of baptism and the Lord's Supper, the Visible Word of God. Most importantly for this writer, God speaks to us through the sermon, the Proclaimed Word of God.

Some may consider the sermon nothing more than the words of a trained theologian and devoted follower of Christ. Historically, however, the Christian Church has viewed the sermon as "not only an exposition of God's Word," but as the "the Word of God addressed to God's people."[2] As the Second Helvitic Confession states, when the Written Word of God is preached, the "very Word of God is proclaimed and received by the faithful."

That, of course, does not mean that preaching is identical with the Word of God. We must view the proclamation of the Word as independent of the subjective character of the person behind the pulpit. "The validity of the proclamation of the Word depends solely on its content; it depends on whether or not the sermon does in fact give expression to God's Word."[3] But we can not leave out the role of the Holy Spirit in this process. Summarizing John Calvin's high view of preaching, Bernard Cooke wrote:

> The minister of the word is the ambassador of Christ, and speaks for him. Yet, at the same time, there is in Calvin's view an unmistakable sacramentality in the preaching of the word. This word is salvific and life-giving because it is accompanied by the power of Christ's own Spirit; in authentic preaching of the word, God makes his saving presence known to believers.[4]

---

[2] Michael Horton, *Rediscovering the Drama of Christ-Centered Worship*, 156.
[3] Jan Rohls, *Reformed Confessions: Theology from Zurich to Barmen*, translated by John Hoffmeyer (Louisville, KY: Westminster John Knox Press, 1998), 178-179.
[4] Bernard Cooke, *Ministry to Word and Sacraments: History and Theology* (Philadelphia: Fortress Press, 1976), 291-292.

The Content of Worship

Since God encounters us in worship through his Word and Spirit, we approach worship with expectation. We come, in short, expecting a Word from the Lord. We gather for worship expecting a "Spirit-charged encounter with God."[5] We come hoping that during our time with God's people, the Holy Spirit – not the liturgy – will shape and mold us into the likeness of Jesus Christ. We come seeking "purposive interaction" with the Lord that leads to inner transformation and fuller "conformity to Christ."[6] In short, we hope to leave the sanctuary different than we arrived for no one can come into the presence of God and remain the same.

Recent efforts at liturgical renewal have enriched the worship of God's people in many ways. However, in my observation, those same efforts have often minimized the role of preaching. Self-proclaimed "seeker" congregations tend to minimize preaching by framing it with dramatic sketches or video clips, and by reducing its content to little more than a list of self-help tips. Mainline congregations, discouraged by legacies of poor preaching, tend to minimize the sermon by over-stating the place of the sacraments. Donald Macleod observed this trend in the Common Order of the Presbyterians where he finds a shift in focus from the sermon to the sacraments. He offers this stinging commentary:

> It is true that the standard of preaching is often disappointing. It is true, too, that the pulpit can be blasphemously abused as an instrument of power and control. It is even true that a very serious issue is raised by the fact that the preacher in a kerygmatic tradition is far more likely to become a "personality" (and thus a barrier to people's seeing Christ) than a priest in a liturgical one. But curtailing and marginalizing preaching is not the answer. Christ was a preacher: the idea of his spending his time going around Palestine administering sacraments is preposterous. It was by preaching that he made an impact and for that preaching that he was finally crucified.[7]

---

[5] Marva J. Dawn, *Reaching Out Without Dumbing Down*, 202.
[6] Dallas Willard, *Renovation of the Heart*, 22-23.
[7] Donald Macleod, "Calvin into Hipplytus," in *To Glorify God: Essays on Modern Reformed Liturgy*, edited by Bryan D. Spinks and Iain R. Torrance (Grand Rapids, MI: Eerdmans Publishing Co, 1999), 260.

Throughout history, however, the Church has viewed preaching as the "supreme task of the church,"[8] an essential mark of the true church, and the core of corporate worship. The liturgy, then, will always dedicate a significant percentage of time to the sermon, the preacher will dedicate a good chunk of time to the preparation of the sermon, and the people will come expecting to receive a faithful exposition of God's Word.

Principle #15 On the Truth in Worship:
We worship the Lord in truth.

> *"A time is coming and has now come when the true worshipers will worship the Father in spirit and truth, for they are the kind of worshipers the Father seeks. God is spirit, and his worshipers must worship in spirit and in truth." (John 4:23-24)*

I remember a time as a teenager when the adults debated the propriety of a hymn called "In the Garden" by C. Austin Miles. The first verse and chorus read:

> I come to the garden alone while the dew is still on the roses;
> And the voice I hear, falling on my ear, the Son of God discloses.
> And He walks with me, and He talks with me, and He tells me I am His own;
> And the joy we share as we tarry there none other has ever known.

Some in my staunchly Reformed congregation thought the song had no place in corporate worship. Their objection focused on the lyrics. In that twentieth-century Christians don't walk with Christ in a garden, opponents thought the hymn should not be sung in our sanctuary. Others thought the hymn stimulated positive emotions about Christ by inviting people back to the time when Christ walked among his disciples. In the end, while "In the Garden" has been a popular hymn among many Protestants, it never made it into our denominationally-approved hymn book.

---

[8] R.B. Kuiper, *The Glorious Body of Christ* (Grand Rapids, MI: Eerdmans Publishing Co.), 163.

The Content of Worship

Some might think that kind of debate foolish, but it reflects an appropriate concern. The debate over "In the Garden" reflected a concern prescribed by Jesus for truthful worship (John 4:24). While one worship service "can never give us the whole truth," in obedience to Christ, the head of the Church, worship planners must insist that not one worship service "give us untruth or less than truth."[9]

The insistence on truthful worship follows the recognition that the liturgy shapes the faith of its participants. I experienced that power first hand. For eighteen years I was nurtured with a liturgy that included the weekly reading of the "Ten Commandments." It wasn't long before I became convinced that, while God did not bring me out of the land of Egypt, the Christian life embraced the Law of Moses. My liturgical experience led be to conclude that the Decalogue was much more important than other aspects of the Christian life, such as the fruit of the Spirit. The liturgy helped create that assumption.

That same liturgy also created an attitude of awe and reverence in my heart for the Lord. During those same eighteen years I entered the sanctuary in silence. That was tough. My parents, who raised five rambunctious children, wanted to be in the sanctuary at least twenty minutes before the service began. So, upon our arrival, we streamed down the center aisle, found "our" pew, and sat down in the same order each week, with my brother and I strategically placed within an arm's length of my father. When asked why we had to arrive so early for church, our parents gave us different reasons. First and foremost, we had to get to church before anyone sat in "our" pew. But as a child I noticed something else going on. I watched my parents prepare themselves for worship. While they would never use the phrase, they "centered down" in the presence of God's people. They reviewed the liturgy, pre-read the Scripture lesson, and read the bulletin. It should not surprise me that today, like my parents, I commit significant time to preparation for the worship of an awesome God.

Liturgy shapes its participants in one way or another. Hence, worship planners must give special attention to every aspect of the liturgy, especially the words. Congregations face a major obstacle in this area: we live in a post-modern context that rejects the notion of objective truth. Still, God calls

---

[9] Marva Dawn, *A Royal Waste of Time: The Splendor of Worshiping God and Being the Church for the World* (Grand Rapids, MI: Eerdmans Publishing, Co., 1999), 68.

us to worship Him in truth. So, while many worshipers remain indifferent to truth, those planning worship bathe the liturgy in truth so that every movement, action, and word finds support in God's Word. More specifically, when it comes to congregational songs, worship planners insist on lyrics that affirm biblical truth as interpreted by their creeds and confessions.

That is not always an easy practice. Many of our congregants listen to "Christian radio" throughout the week. They listen to some songs that have biblical lyrics but, for one reason or another, are not appropriate for worship. Plus, they listen to some songs with beautiful melodies but less than truthful lyrics. When these radio-listening congregants come to "church," they ask those planning worship to insert some of these songs in the liturgy. When the worship planners decline, they receive labels like "elitist." But there is no small issue at stake here. We have been called to worship the Lord in truth.

For many years, congregations sang only from denominationally approved hymn books. That practice insured worship planners that the songs included in the book had passed both theological and aesthetic tests. In recent years, however, we have experienced an explosion of sacred music, accompanied by an explosion in technology whereby Christians have quick access to the newest sacred music. Since it takes many years for a denomination to produce song books, many congregations have chosen not to wait for official sanction before incorporating new songs into their liturgical lives. When such a step is taken, worship planners, committed to truth in worship, should carefully examine the lyrics of songs before inviting worshipers to sing them. They don't want to introduce songs so light on truth that they could be sung at a night club, nor utilize "songs with cheap or sentimental lyrics or banal music that belie the coherence and integrity of God."[10] They want to employ songs that convey the rich truth about the great God we worship.

Delegating the responsibility of planning worship to a person or group of people forms a second challenge for most congregations. This group often includes musicians, since they play a vital role in worship, but should also include individuals who think biblically about worship and who have the gift of theological discernment. Such individuals may help the group distinguish between "personal liturgical agendas," on one side,

---

[10] Marva Dawn, *A Royal Waste of Time*, 67.

and appropriate elements for corporate worship, on the other.[11] Without them, worship committees often implement the latest fads, even when they fail to support the theological convictions of the congregation.

Of course, no matter how intense or sincere the efforts of those planning worship, our liturgies will always include imperfection. As Paul said, "now we see but a poor reflection" (I Corinthians 13:10). Our understanding is limited, as is our faith. We can only hope that the Lord, whom we seek to worship in truth, will, by the power of the Holy Spirit, compensate for our weaknesses. Towards that hope, we pray constantly that the Lord will work in spite of and through our imperfections.

Principle #16 On the Drama of Worship: Worship includes the sacraments.

"Do this in remembrance of me." (I Corinthians 11:24)

I enjoy the performing arts. As a high school student, I participated in a couple plays, as well as a musical. As a college student, I loved playing in the Wind Ensemble and Jazz Band. While a college chaplain, I enjoyed each and every dramatic production by the students. As a Chicagoan, I have taken advantage of a wide spectrum of performing arts. But, I have yet to propose the inclusion of dramatic sketches in worship. While this practice has considerable support in self-described "seeker-sensitive" congregations, it has never done much for me.

I realize that is a subjective response, but I have yet to discover an objective biblical case for the inclusion of dramatic sketches in worship. While the apostle Paul assures us that God has gifted the congregation with preachers, he doesn't mention actors. That same apostle assures us that salvation comes through the preaching of the Gospel, but he doesn't promise the effectiveness of dramatic sketches. There is nothing in Scripture to suggest we should even consider such an innovation in worship. In fact, by its silence on this matter, we find just the opposite. Ed Clowney writes,

---

[11] John D. Witvliet, "A Discerning Spirit: Making Good Choices in an Era of Liturgical Change," *Books and Culture* (September/October 2003), 22-26.

Principled Worship

In the New Testament times, drama was staged in the major centers of the Hellenistic world and was immensely popular. The apostles, however, delivered the urgent gospel message in direct teaching and preaching, not through the indirect communication of dramatic performance. We recognize the need for direct communication in situations of supreme seriousness. An American president would not air a dramatic skit to appeal for national support in a declaration of war.[12]

If a congregation, however, insists on drama in worship, I suggest it embrace the sacraments. Interestingly, among the plethora of books which promote dramatic sketches in worship few propose a greater appreciation of the sacraments, the visible signs and dramatic seals of God's grace to us in Christ.[13] There have been exceptions, most notably, those who have traveled the "road to Canterbury."[14] But an overview of literature on worship in recent decades reveals a general neglect of the significance of the Lord's Supper and baptism in worship among Evangelicals.

New Testament worship, however, in obedience to the commands of Christ, included at least two liturgical actions that many Christians refer to as sacraments: baptism (Matthew 28:18-20) and the "breaking of bread" or the Lord's Supper (Acts 2:42-47). Granted, as Leonard Vander Zee notes, "the New Testament does not offer a well-defined concept of sacraments as such;" but baptism and the Lord's Supper "occur as rites that the church performs at Christ's command and by the power of the Holy Spirit to incorporate converts into Christ and his church by baptism, and remember their fellowship with Christ and with each other in the supper."[15]

The interpretation of those two rites has divided Christians into two camps. The first group includes those who describe the Lord's Supper and baptism as ordinances that merely symbolize the redemptive work of

---

[12] Edmund P. Clowney, *The Church*, 127.
[13] John Calvin, *Institutes of Christian Religion* 4.14.1.
[14] Robert Webber, *Evangelicals on the Canterbury Trail: Why Evangelicals Are Attracted to the Liturgical Church* (Word Publishing: Jarrell Imprint, 1985).
[15] Leonard Vander Zee, *Christ, Baptism and the Lord's Supper: Recovering the Sacraments for Evangelical Worship* (Downers Grove, IL: InterVarsity Press, 2004), 44.

The Content of Worship

Christ and, as such, trigger greater devotion by the participant for Christ. The second group, of which I am a part, describes the Lord's Supper and baptism as sacraments. We believe that they are "visible signs of invisible grace," as Augustine noted, which do more than jar our memories. They also serve as vessels of God's grace to us His people. The Heidelberg Catechism offers a splendid summary of the meaning and purpose of the sacraments in "Lord's Day 25":

> Sacraments are holy signs and seals for us to see. They were instituted by God so that by our use of them he might make us understand more clearly the promise of the gospel, and might put his seal on that promise. And this is God's gospel promise: to forgive our sins and give us eternal life by grace alone because of Christ's one sacrifice finished on the cross.

In summary, we believe that God has given us the sacraments "as a means of strengthening our faith in Christ, assuring us, and delivering his blessing."[16]

Leonard Vander Zee nicely summarizes how the sacraments accomplish such lofty objectives.[17] He breaks down their action into four parts: (1) By the Holy Spirit, "we are united with Jesus Christ in the sacraments through the Holy Spirit." (2) God imparts His gracious salvation in Christ to us through the physical elements and ritual action of the sacraments. "God uses physical elements to convey spiritual reality." (3) Sacraments impart God's grace in Christ to us when these physical elements are joined to the word. The sacraments and the word belong together; they "confirm the word through our senses." (4) The sacraments are received through faith. While faith does not make the sacraments effective, "they do not benefit those who do not receive them in faith and obedience."

---

[16] Michael Horton, *A Better Way: Rediscovering Christ-Centered Worship*, 44.

[17] Leonard Vander Zee, *Christ, Baptism and the Lord's Supper*, 53-69.

[18] D. Marion Clark, "Baptism: Joyful Sign of the Gospel," in *Give Praise to God: A Vision For Reforming Worship*, edited by Philip Graham Ryken, Derek W.H. Thomas, and J. Ligon Duncan III (Phillipsburg, PA: P&R Publishing, Inc, 2003), 170.

[19] *Worship Sourcebook*, 249.

Principled Worship

The sacrament of incorporation is baptism, "God's gift to his church to fill his people with joy."[18] It is a "a physical, ritual action, mandated by Jesus, through which God acts to nourish, sustain, comfort, challenge, teach, and assure us."[19] Through baptism God says, "You belong to me." That truth, as the Heidelberg Catechism notes in its first Lord's Day, is our "only comfort in both life and in death." Believers are baptized once, but the event has several layers of meaning. "It is at once a sign of the washing away of sin, a sign of our union with Jesus' death and resurrection, a sign of the promise of new birth in Christ, a sign of incorporation in the church, a sign of the promise of the Holy Spirit, and a sign of the covenant and kingdom of God."[20] Since it signals incorporation into the Church, it is a communal, not a private or family act. It is administered by a representative of the gathering community and in the presence of that same community.

The sacrament of the Lord's Supper is also "a physical, ritual action, mandated by Jesus, through which God acts to nourish, sustain, comfort, challenge, teach, and assure us."[21] The New Testament describes the Lord's Supper as a feast of "remembrance, communion, and hope."[22] By eating the bread and drinking the cup, we not only remember our redemption in Jesus Christ through his death on the cross and gain renewed hope for that day when we will enjoy a wedding feast in heaven, but we commune with Christ (I Corinthians 10:17). The nineteenth-century Reformed theologian John Nevin, echoing the sentiments of John Calvin, describes this communion through the Lord's Supper as a "real participation" with Christ.[23] Clarifying his position Nevin writes, "In the Lord's Supper the believer communicates not only with the Spirit of Christ, or with his divine nature, but with Christ himself in his whole living person; so that he may be said to be fed and nourished by his very flesh and blood."[24]

Personally, I don't understand how Christ is present in the Lord's Supper. I don't understand how he nourishes my soul through the eating of bread and drinking of grape juice. But because the Bible is the

---

[20] *Worship Sourcebook*, 249.
[21] *Worship Sourcebook*, 305-306.
[22] In *The Liturgy of the Reformed Church in America*, 64.
[23] John W. Nevin, *The Mystical Presence* (New York: Garland Publishing, Inc., 1987), 55.
[24] John W. Nevin, *The Mystical Presence*, 58.

inspired Word of God, I acknowledge that mystery as true. I believe that participation in the Lord's Supper is communion with Christ, who is my life, light, righteousness, wisdom, knowledge, sanctification, and redemption. Hence, through participation in the sacrament of the Lord's Supper I grow in grace in a way I would not otherwise grow. Through Him I become more like him. John Calvin describes that benefit in this way:

> In (the Lord's Supper) we have a witness of our growth into one body with Christ such that whatever is his may be called ours.... This is the wonderful exchange he has made with us; that, becoming Son of man with us, he has made us sons of God with him; that, by his descent to earth, he has prepared an ascent to heaven for us; that, by taking on our mortality, he has conferred his immortality upon us; that, accepting our weakness, he has strengthened us by his power; that, receiving our poverty unto himself, he has transferred his wealth to us; that, taking the weight of our iniquity upon himself, he has clothed us with his righteousness.[25]

That understanding of the Lord's Supper promotes both decisive preparation by the worshiper and frequent participation. With respect to preparation, we examine ourselves before eating the bread and drinking the cup because we do not want to participate in the sacrament in an "unworthy manner" (I Corinthians 11:27-28). We also warn one another that any one who comes to the table with unrepentant sins "eats and drinks judgment" on him or herself (I Corinthians 11:29). With respect to the frequency of participation, our convictions about the Lord's Supper suggest that we receive the Lord's Supper often, perhaps even weekly. After all, we believe that the Lord's Supper offers us grace that we can't receive anywhere else since, through participation in the Supper, Christ mystically and really presents himself and his benefits to us.

Our ecclesiastical experience, however, has encouraged us to limit the number of times we receive the Lord's Supper. One argument has been that an increased frequency diminishes our appreciation for it. Another argument, closely linked to the practice of church discipline, states that

---

[25] John Calvin, *Institutes of Christian Religion* IV.17.2.

the Sacrament is so special that it requires significant preparation, so much so that one could not participate in weekly Communion without "eating and drinking" judgment on self. Congregations of such a mind may offer the Lord's Supper as few as four times a year.

Each congregation must wrestle with the issue of frequency, finding a place at or within the two poles of weekly celebration and quarterly. It seems to me that no fault can be found with any congregation that subscribes to the weekly celebration of the Lord's Supper. Such a practice rests on a strong biblical and theological foundation. It also responds to the yearnings of a new generation of Christians who long for visible and sensual elements in worship. Those offering the sacrament as infrequently as four times a year, however, stand on shaky ground.

In summary, those planning worship will find a place for the drama of the sacraments not only because Christ has mandated those rites, but because our faith, like the light of a lantern, diminishes without the oil of God's grace. Our faith grows faint without nourishment and exercise. We become weak. Like Peter, we deny the Lord. Like Thomas, we doubt the Lord. Like David, we disobey the Lord. Without spiritual nourishment for our souls, the stress and strain of life frays our faith and glazes our love. We need the nourishment of Jesus Christ who is the Bread of Life and who offers the only water that quenches our thirst. Through the operation of the Holy Spirit, coupled with faith, the sacraments nourish our souls, for it is by grace we believe and by grace we continue to believe.

Principle #17 On the Prayers of Worship: Worship includes prayer.

They devoted themselves to the apostles' teaching and to the fellowship, to the breaking of bread and to prayer." (Acts 2:42)

I once served a congregation in the Reformed tradition that, like each of the Fundamentalist congregations in the neighborhood, had a mid-week prayer meeting. Each Wednesday night a couple dozen church members gathered for prayer, or so it was said. During my tenure, the prayer meeting was never well attended. That fact didn't please the unofficial elders of the congregation who measured the congregation's spiritual maturity, not

The Content of Worship

by how many came to morning worship, or by how many who came to evening worship, but by how many came to mid-week prayer meeting. The faithful attendees encouraged me to preach on mid-week service attendance, but I couldn't find a text to go with that sermon.

Truth be told, I wasn't a big fan of the mid-week prayer meeting for one reason: we didn't pray much. The hour included a couple songs, a thirty minute lesson from Scripture, and prayer requests, more often than not, for those not in attendance who happened to be suffering from any number of medical conditions. Then, the meeting concluded with a few minutes of "popcorn" prayer, with the same few people popping up and praying each week. It seemed to me at that time and to this day, that the real prayer meeting took place every Sunday morning. Our weekly worship service included a lot more prayer than any of our mid-week prayer meetings.

It seems to me we may accurately describe the weekly gathering of a covenanted community as a prayer meeting. Like the First Church in Jerusalem, our liturgy includes prayer, a lot of prayer. *The Worship Sourcebook*, co-published in 2004 by the Calvin Institute of Christian Worship, Faith Alive Christian Resources (a ministry of CRC Publications), and Baker Books, offers an outstanding catalogue of liturgical prayers. In that excellent volume, the editors identify and describe several types of prayers, including:

> Opening Prayers or Invocations - In this type of prayer we invoke or call upon the Lord, acknowledge God's promised presence and affirm "that the power in worship is a gift from God rather than a human accomplishment."[26]

> Prayers of Confession - In this type of prayer we seek God's forgiveness for our sins.

> Prayers for Illumination – In this type of prayer, offered at the beginning of a service, or before the reading of Scripture, or before the sermon, we acknowledge that sin limits our understanding, hardens our hearts,

---

[26] *The Worship Sourcebook*, 68.

and blurs our vision. Then, we seek God's grace to overcome our deficiencies.

Prayers of the People – In this type of prayer we intercede for "the congregation, for people we know, for those in authority, for those suffering oppression, for those who are poor, hungry, or sick, and so on."[27]

Offering Prayers - Through this type of prayer we frame the offering of money by acknowledging God as the giver of all good gifts and "that money itself cannot accomplish good in the world without God's blessing."[28]

In recent worship services, you may have offered most of those prayers, as well as a couple others. Plus, you may have prayed in one or more modes: silently and audibly, spoken and sung, by one and by some and by all, in unison and as a responsive reading (antiphonal). Wouldn't you agree that we may describe the weekly gathering of God's people as a prayer meeting?

Prayer holds a prominent place in the liturgy for several reasons. First, our identity prompts prayer. We are the adopted children of God through the finished work of Jesus Christ. Our loving Father in heaven invites us to seek His grace in prayer (John 14:13-14,15:7-8,16:23,24). Second, obedience prompts prayer. We pray because God has mandated faithful (Romans 12:12) and continuous prayer (I Thessalonians 5:17). To not pray would be an act of disobedience. Third, we pray out of gratitude. God's grace so fills our hearts that words burst forth with praise and thanksgiving. Like the Psalmist, our mouths offer prayers of praise. Finally, we pray because we need help in this broken world. From time to time, the burdens and disappointments of life bring us to our knees. At His invitation, we call upon the Lord in our days of trouble (Psalm 50:15).

Occasionally our faith falters and we pray without hope (James 1:5-8). Instead of praying with confidence for the unimaginable blessings of God, we limit our requests to "traveling mercies," to blessings on food, and to

---

[27] *The Worship Sourcebook*, 173.
[28] *The Worship Sourcebook*, 240.

healing through surgeries. Our faltering faith hinders us from praying about the deepest concerns of our lives. We hesitate because somewhere, beneath our surface layer of religiosity, we don't believe God has the power to do anything about them. "Consequently nothing," states Martin Luther, "is so necessary as to call upon God incessantly and drum into his ears our prayer that He may give, preserve, and increase in us faith and obedience… and remove all that stands in our way and hinders us."

During nearly thirty years of pastoral ministry, I have made many mistakes in my public prayer ministry. The biggest mistake was a failure to prepare my liturgical prayers. Thankfully, somewhere along the line, a fellow pastor asked this question: "In most of our worship services we pray as much we preach, but how much time do we commit to preparing our prayers?" That question struck a nerve. I had been trained to spend ten to twenty hours a week preparing one sermon, but occasionally ran into the pulpit and prayed extemporaneously. Now, I write and read most of my prayers.

Like many pastors, I find inspiration from the prayers of others. Sometimes I borrow their prayers, giving credit where credit is due. More often, the prayers of others inspire paraphrases or something new. Looking back, I have discovered a residual blessing from that practice. It has kept my prayers fresh and unpredictable, which is very important for long-term resident pastors. Plus, it has helped build a memory bank of prayers from which to draw upon during those inevitable opportunities when God's people call upon their pastor for an extemporaneous prayer.

Principle #18 On the Gospel in Worship: Worship is evangelistic.

> *How, then, can they call on the one they have not believed in?*
> *And how can they believe in the one of whom they have not heard?*
> *And how can they hear without someone preaching to them?*
> *And how can they preach unless they are sent? As it is written, "How beautiful are the feet of those who bring good news." (Romans 10:14-15)*

Christians embrace and live with tension. We affirm both God's sovereignty and human responsibility. We affirm salvation by the kind of faith that works. We treasure life on earth while longing for life in heaven. We live in the world, but are not of it. We seek to transform the world, submitting it to the Lordship of Christ, knowing the Lord will come again and destroy it. We affirm that Christ has already established his reign on earth, but not yet fully. We wrestle simultaneously with the influence of our sinful nature and that of the Holy Spirit. We pray as if everything depends on God and work as if everything depends on our efforts.

Tension also characterizes our weekly corporate gatherings. First, the liturgy represents tension between the past and the present, old forms and new ones, the organ and the guitar, the ancient psalms and new scripture songs. While the church regularly updates its forms, the pace upon which the new is integrated with the old, and the prominence either is given, provides anxiety, if not tension, for many. Second, the expectations for the weekly gathering create tension. Christians expect both an opportunity to worship the Lord and the effectual preaching of the Gospel. In particular, they hope that believers will grow in the "grace and knowledge of the Lord," and that unbelievers in the congregation, both members and visitors alike, will come to saving faith in Christ. As a result, in one corporate body, on any given Sunday morning, we will find Christians who long to praise the Lord for His grace, as well as awakened sinners who long to know the grace of God in Christ. Theoretically, then, our weekly worship service includes opportunity for both worship and evangelism, sanctification and justification.

Throughout the history of the American Protestant Church, Christians have relieved that tension by designing and implementing special services to reach the un-churched. My generation has witnessed services led by gifted evangelists like Billy Graham and Luis Palau. More recently, we have witnessed the remarkable ministry of Bill Hybels and others in the "Seeker-Sensitive Movement." God has used special services to lead many individuals to saving faith in Jesus Christ. But, while they have a place in the life of the church, they do not replace the tried and true evangelistic method of corporate worship.

Corporate worship includes believers who seek the Lord in worship, as well as awakened sinners who will inevitably seek the Lord in faith. The presence of the awakened within the gathered explains why the liturgy is evangelistic. It explains why, for centuries, individuals, prompted by the Holy Spirit, have attended corporate worship, listened to a preacher, called on the name of the Lord, and come to saving faith – just as the apostle Paul foretold in Romans 10:13-14:

> Everyone who calls on the name of the Lord will be saved. How, then, can they call on the one they have not believed in? And how can they believe in the one of whom they have not heard? And how can they hear without someone preaching to them?

Stanley Hauerwas wrote, "Worship has always been the way the Church has both evangelized and gone about its moral formation."[29] John Calvin taught that the preaching of the Word has one final objective: to bring the listener to faith.[30] One branch of Presbyterianism in America states,

> Evangelism is God's people joyfully sharing the good news of the sovereign love of God and God's Spirit calling all people to repentance, to personal faith in Jesus Christ as Savior and Lord, to active membership in the church, and to obedient service and witness in the world.[31]

Since worship is evangelistic, congregations should expect the gathered community to include "seekers" who have been prepared by God's Spirit to claim Christ in faith, and should expect the effectual preaching of the Word. This does not mean we should not implement supplemental evangelistic programs. It is, however, to assert that we need not take an either-or approach to the weekly gathering of God's people. Through God's sovereign and mysterious work, the same worship service will lead Christians to maturity and unbelievers to faith. As R.B. Kuiper wrote, "Through His Word God both gives faith to those who have it not and strengthens the faith of those who have it."[32]

---

[29] Stanley Hauerwas, "Worship, Evangelism, Ethics: On Eliminating the 'And'," in *Liturgy and the Moral Self,* 97.

[30] W. Niesel, *The Theology of John Calvin* (Philadelphia: Fortress Press, 1956), 26-30, 120-125.

[31] From the Evangelism Office of the Presbyterian Church.

[32] R.B. Kuiper, *The Glorious Body of Christ*, 201.

Principle #19 On the Praise of Worship:
Worship includes praise.

"Praise the Lord. Praise, O servants of the Lord, praise the name of the Lord. Let the name of the Lord be praised, both now and forevermore."
(Psalm 113:1-2)

As a kid, I remember my parents and grandparents referring to the stuff before the sermon as the "preliminaries." They understood every liturgical act leading up to the sermon as prelude. They believed that "going to church" was basically about hearing a sermon. Everything else was secondary. With that mindset dominating most of the 20th century American-Evangelical landscape, worship became, as A.W. Tozer once noted, a "missing jewel" from the weekly gathering of many congregations.

One of the more significant developments in the last quarter of a century has been the conviction that "going to church" involves more than the sermon; it also affords us an opportunity to offer our praise to the Lord. Christians have defined and described the praise of our Triune God in a variety of ways. Everett Harrison defines it as those actions by which we denote the "worthiness of a person to receive special honor in accordance with that worth; in a narrow sense worship is pure adoration."[33] John Calvin taught that in praise we acknowledge our Triune God as "the only source of virtue, justice, holiness, wisdom, truth, power, goodness, mercy, life, and salvation;" in our praise we "ascribe and render to him the glory of all that is good!"[34] Gerald B. Stanton defines praise as "homage rendered to God by his creatures in worship of his person and in thanksgiving for his favors and blessings."[35] However we describe it, each week the liturgy offers believers an opportunity to "exalt His name together" (Psalm 34:3) and "declare the praise of God who has called (them) out of darkness into His marvelous light" (I Peter 2:9).

---

[33] Everett F. Harrison, "Worship," *Evangelical Dictionary of Theology* (Grand Rapids, MI: Baker Book House, 1984), 1192.
[34] John Calvin, *The Necessity of Reforming the Church* (Dallas, TX: Protestant Heritage Series, 1995), 16.
[35] Gerald B. Stanton, "Praise," *Evangelical Dictionary of Theology* (Grand Rapids, MI: Baker Book House, 1984), 865.

The Content of Worship

The common denominator to each of those definitions of worship is content. Each one insists on describing the qualities of God which prompt our praise. We may occasionally limit our praise to "Hallelujah" or "Praise the Lord" or "I Love You, Lord." Normally, however, our praise joyfully describes the attributes and enumerates the blessings which prompt our praise. In other words, praise includes words by which we ascribe glory to our Triune God.

Christians long for this opportunity because the grace of God in Christ prompts gratitude. With the Psalmist we proclaim, "Better is one day with God's people in praise, than a thousand days elsewhere" (Psalm 84:10). As guilty sinners saved by grace and filled with the Spirit, we wish to "waste our time immersed in all the fullness of God's splendor."[36]

God does not leave us without coaching on how to offer our praise. Psalm 100, for example, teaches us to blend reverence and fear with shouting and singing. In Luke 1, Mary, the mother of Jesus, models humility in worship as she acknowledges her unworthiness to birth the Messiah. In Psalm 145, David reminds us to look beyond the gifts to the giver by not only thanking the Lord for His blessings, but by praising Him for His greatness, goodness, glory and grace.

While corporate praise is an end in itself, it bears fruit in our lives. First, by joining our hearts, minds and lips together in praise, we express our unity as the body of Christ. The Reformers, for example, preferred congregational singing in unison, without instruments, to accent both the human voice and the unity of the congregation. E. Byron Anderson writes,

> As a practice by which persons express personal and communal faith, hymn singing physically and mentally situates the person in a context of relatedness to the whole of a community whose voice is united in song and to God.[37]

---

[36] Marva Dawn, *A Royal Waste of Time*, 343.
[37] E. Byron Anderson, "O for a heart to praise my God,' Hymning the Self Before God," in *Liturgy and the Moral Self*, edited by E Byron Anderson and Bruce T. Morrill (Collegeville: MN, The Liturgical Press, 1998), 120.

Second, it nourishes the soul of the worshiper. Praise soothes the heart and confirms the faith of the believer. Tears often flow, for example, when lyrics draw out memories of God's gracious help in time of need.

> The singing of a hymn is more than making music, more than a nice song filling dead space in a liturgy, more than an aesthetic act, more than an act of self-expression. It is an act of pastoral care in times of need and rejoicing.[38]

Third, praise fulfills one aspect of God's will for our lives and, thereby, sanctifies us.[39] On over fifty occasions in the Psalms alone, God commands his people to worship Him. Since God mandates worship, our praise may viewed as an act of obedience, one that leads to spiritual formation, for during corporate worship, God's people are "stirred up to more and more genuine devotion to God."[40]

Fourth, praise allows us to engage in the highest activity in heaven and on earth. Inventors have given us remarkable discoveries. Writers have compiled many volumes of excellent literature. Singers have spellbound their audiences. Artists have mesmerized those who witness their work. Presidents and kings have changed the course of history. But none of the world's greatest men and women has ever done anything half as great as when believers praise the Lord. None has done anything so noble as to give God a few minutes of glorious praise.

---

[38] E. Byron Anderson, "O for a heart to praise my God," 11.
[39] Howard L. Rice & James C. Huffstutler, *Reformed Worship*, 195.
[40] Hughes Oliphant Old, *Worship Reformed According to Scripture*, 46.

Chapter Five
The Music of Worship

Principle #20 On the Songs of Worship:
There is no worship without song.

> *"Come, let us sing for joy to the Lord; let us shout aloud to the Rock of our salvation. Let us come before him with thanksgiving, and extol him with music and song. For the Lord is the great God, the great King above all gods." (Psalm 95:1-3)*

I have not yet worshiped with a community of believers whose liturgy does not include song. It seems that when God's people come together, someone sings. A soloist may offer a song of testimony or confession of sin. A choir may offer a song of praise or thanksgiving. A congregation may sing a psalm or hymn. At one time or another, I have heard nearly every element on the worship service brought forth in song.

Song is especially prominent for Christians as a form of praise. We may speak words of praise, perhaps through a unison reading of a Psalm or by a spontaneous "Hallelujah." We may accompany our spoken words with the clapping of hands (Psalm 47:1), or with the lifting of our hands (Psalm 63:4), or even with dancing (Psalm 149:3). We may offer silent prayers of praise in response to the ministry of the church choir or a soloist; in such circumstances our lips remain silent while our hearts burst forth in praise (Psalm 4:7). But the primary manner in which we offer our praise is through song.

We sing three types of songs: "psalms, hymns and spiritual songs" (Colossians 3:16). While biblical scholars have sound reason to refer to many passages in scripture as "psalms," I prefer, for educational purposes, to limit my use of the term as a reference to the one hundred and fifty recorded in the Old Testament Psalter. Psalm singing has a rich heritage, especially among Reformed Christians, some of whom still limit corporate song to the Psalms. John Calvin, among others, believed that the best way to assure truthful worship is to sing the Psalms. My congregation's song book, *The Psalter Hymnal*, includes at least one melodic rendering of each Old Testament Psalm. Personally, I would find it difficult to describe our worship as Reformed if it did not include at least one Psalm.

The Greek word *hymnos* refers to songs in praise of the gods or of a hero. Augustine narrowly defined a hymn as a song of praise to God, but that definition seems too narrow.[1] Hughes Oliphant Old offers a content-driven definition of a hymn: "an elaboration, a sort of drawing out, a commentary, or perhaps a sort of meditation" on the Lord and His Word.[2] Stephen Marini adds that a hymn must not only convey "belief content," but also be presented with "sacred intentionality."[3] Combining Old and Marini, I suggest that we may define a hymn as a song whose lyrics comment on the Lord and His Word, and whose style is appropriate for worship. While that definition may allow for too much subjectivity, it does highlight the two critical ingredients of a hymn: content and purpose.

The Christian Church has been singing hymns since its inception. Biblical scholars have identified the lyrics of several early Christian hymns in Scripture, most notably, Philippians 2:5-11. Hymn singing has been very popular among Protestants, especially since the days of Jonathan Edwards. Today, Christians use the hymn as a tool for praise, confession of sin, profession of faith, thanksgiving, and affirmation.

---

[1] Augustine, *Comment on Psalm 148*.
[2] Hughes Oliphant Old, *Worship Reformed According to Scripture*, 35.
[3] Stephen A. Marini, *Sacred Song in America: Religion, Music, Public Culture* (Champaign, IL: University of Illinois, 2003), 7.

There is no consensus as to the exact nature of "spiritual songs." Right or wrong, I have found it helpful in planning worship to describe Scripture songs (other than the Psalms) as spiritual songs. This genre of sacred song is often characterized by redundancy and simplicity. It is especially popular as a teaching tool with children. Many of us learned at a young age, for example, that the wise man built his "house upon the rock."

American Protestants, and perhaps others, have experienced an explosion of spiritual songs in recent years, typically referred to as "praise and worship" music. While many have attacked this recent phenomenon, I appreciate Hughes Oliphant Old's balanced perspective:

> It is of the very nature of American Protestantism that the ministry of praise is so central to its worship and flows forth so abundantly and in such rich variety. This should not surprise us. We have often seen this happen before. The ministry of praise wells up from the grass roots of Christian faith. It is a folk art, inspired by the Holy Spirit, and comes naturally in its own time.[4]

During the past decade or two, we have witnessed an explosion of sacred music, most of which is readily accessible to the people in the pews through radio and internet. At the same time, we have witnessed liturgical renewal throughout American Protestantism. Consequently, as we begin another century, we have countless sacred readings and songs available for use in worship. How do we navigate through all the options? Several scholars have come forward in recent years to provide helpful tools for those responsible for selecting music for the liturgy. Marva Dawn, for one, suggests we ask the following questions:

Is the text theologically sound?

Does the style disrupt worship in any way?

How appropriate is the piece with respect to our goal to use music for the diversity of congregation members?

---

[4] Hughes Oliphant Old, *Worship Reformed According to Scripture*, 56-57.

Principled Worship

Is this piece of music characterized by excellence and greatness?[5]

Emily Brink and John Witvliet offer four guiding principles for the selection of liturgical music. They believe that it should (1) serve to enact the relationship we have with God in Christ, (2) be common to all the people, (3) have theological integrity, and (4) be in, but not of, the culture of the people.[6] Frank Burch Brown offers a list of assumptions that could fruitfully guide discussions about aesthetic taste in general, and the selection of liturgical music in particular.[7]

> There are many kinds of good religious art and music. In view of cultural diversity, it would be extremely odd if that were not true.
>
> Not all kinds of good art and music are equally good for worship. It is not enough that a work or style of art be likeable; it must be appropriate.
>
> There are various appropriately Christian modes of mediating religious experience artistically – from transcendent to immanent in a sense of the sacred, from abundant to minimal means, from prophetic to pastoral in tone; from instructive to meditative in aim.
>
> Every era and cultural context develops new forms of sacred music and art, which to begin with often seem secular to many people.
>
> No one person can make equally discerning judgments about every kind of music or art. Yet almost everyone is inclined to assume or act otherwise.
>
> It is an act of Christian love to learn to appreciate or at least respect what others value in a particular style or work that they cherish in

---

[5] Marva J. Dawn, *Reaching Out Without Dumbing Down*, 202.
[6] Emily R. Brink and John D. Witvliet, "Music in Reformed Churches Worldwide," *Christian Worship in Reformed Churches Past and Present*, edited by Lukas Vischer (Grand Rapids, MI: Eerdmans Publishing Co., 2003), 339-347.
[7] Frank Burch Brown, *Good Taste, Bad Taste, and Christian Taste: Aesthetics in the Religious Life* (New York: Oxford University Press, 2000), 250-251.

worship. That is different, however, from personally liking every form of commendable art, which is impossible and unnecessary.

Disagreements over taste in religious music or any other art can be healthy and productive; but they touch on sensitive matters and often reflect or embody religious differences as well as aesthetic ones.

The reasons why an aesthetic work or style is good or bad, weak or strong, can never be expressed in words, yet they can often be pointed out through comparative – and repeated – looking and listening.

Aesthetic judgments begin with the community or tradition to which a given style or work is indigenous or most familiar. But they seldom end there; and they cannot, if the style or work is to invite the attention of a wide range of people over a period of time.

The overall evaluation of any art used in worship needs to be a joint effort between clergy, congregation, and trained artists and musicians, taking into account the aesthetic qualities of the art and the requirements of the liturgy.

The congregation benefits from "classic" art or music that challenges and solicits spiritual and theological growth in the aesthetic dimension.

In my congregation, the application of such principles and assumptions has led us to offer psalms, hymns and spiritual songs in a variety of flavors. In any given service, we may sing a Psalm of David set to a nineteenth-

---

[8] Isaac Watts, a Calvinist clergyman, suggested that it was not necessary to limit congregational singing to exact biblical words, i.e., the Psalms. "He promoted the singing of hymns and spiritual songs based on scriptural themes. On this principle he wrote hymns for private devotional use, publishing them as *Hymns and Spiritual Songs* in 1707." See George Marsden, *Jonathan Edwards A Life* (New Haven: Yale University Press, 2003), 144.

[9] The worship wars of the American Protestant Church in the early eighteenth century debated the propriety of "regular" singing, or singing in parts. Jonathan Edwards, among others, encouraged his congregation to embrace the "beauties of regular singing." See George Marsden, *Jonathan Edwards A Life*, 144-145.

century tune, an eighteenth-century hymn by Isaac Watts,[8] and a 1971 chorus by André Crouch. We encourage the congregation to sing in parts by providing written music with all four parts.[9] We try to stay away from songs in the first person singular, believing that such lyrics contradict the corporate nature of our worship. Finally, we offer our praise to the Lord in both a participatory and representative manner. In other words, we not only offer our praise as a congregation. Sometimes a soloist or choir will offer praise on our behalf.

Of course, we have made many mistakes along the way. In my experience, most of them have come as a result of extending hospitality to guests or by uncritically accepting the ministry of volunteers. A mother, for example, volunteers her child, young or old, as a minister of music. The worship planners graciously slot the guest in worship as "special music," only to discover, during the service, that the lyrics of his or her song contradict their theological convictions. Some might conclude from such an experience that they need to approve every song incorporated into the liturgy. No one could debate the propriety of such a decision. Personally, however, I lean to less oversight. I error on the side of grace, at least, that's what I call it, perhaps as a tool to justify my lack of courage to disappoint someone. But I also hope and pray that the Holy Spirit will compensate for inevitable mistakes. If they are the exception, rather than the norm, perhaps the Lord will allow the congregation to receive the offerings of our fellow brothers and sisters in Christ, identify any biblical or theological shortcomings, channel concerns in a positive manner, and still give praise to God.

Principle #21 On the Sounds of Worship:
There is no worship without sound.

> *"Praise God with the sounding of the trumpet, praise him with the harp and lyre, praise him with tambourine and dancing, praise him with the strings and flute, praise him with the clash of cymbals, praise him with resounding cymbals." (Psalm 150:3-5)*

Musical instruments are a wonderful gift to humanity from God. For most Christian churches, they fulfill an important function in the liturgy of His people. There are, of course, a few exceptions. The followers of Thomas and Alexander Campbell, for one, worship without instruments.[10] But for the most part, when the people of God gather, we play our instruments and raise our voices in song. Karl Barth writes,

> The Christian community sings. It is not a choral society. Its singing is not a concert. But from inner, material necessity it sings. Singing is the highest form of human expression… The praise of God which finds its concrete culmination in the singing of the community is one of the indispensable basic forms of the ministry of the community.[11]

Music serves several liturgical functions. It may, as a prelude, create the appropriate atmosphere for one or more segments of the liturgy. It may, as a choral anthem, accompany the prayers of the people. It may, as a vocal solo, accompany a personal testimony about God's grace. It may, as an instrumental piece, serve as an offering to the Lord. The primary function of music, however, is to support congregational song. Through melodies, and with instruments, we worship the Lord by the singing of psalms, hymns and spiritual songs.

Before we add music to the liturgy, however, we should acknowledge its tremendous power. Music, like electricity, can kill you if handled inappropriately. John Calvin offered this assessment:

> We know from experience that song has large power and vigor to move and inflame the heart of man to vehemently call upon and praise God with an ardent, passionate zeal. It has a secret, almost incredible force to move our hearts in one way or another.[12]

---

[10] Followers of Thomas Campbell (1763-1854) and his son, Alexander (1788-1866), believed that since the New Testament does not prescribe or exemplify worship with instruments, Christians should worship without their aid.

[11] Karl Barth, *Church Dogmatics: The Doctrine of Reconciliation*, IV.3.2, translated by G.W. Bromiley (London: T&T Clark, 1961), 866-867.

[12] From John Calvin's preface to his 1542 "Form of Prayers and Ecclesiastical Chants With the Manner of Administering the Sacraments and of Solemnizing Marriage According to Customs of the Ancient Church." A similar quote may be found in Calvin's "Forward to the Psalter," in *John Calvin: Writings on Pastoral Piety*, The Classics of Western Spirituality (New York: Paulist Press, 2001), 94.

Since music has an incredible force to move our hearts in a variety of ways, we acknowledge that some styles of music may not be appropriate for corporate worship. As Michael Horton and others point out, style is not neutral.[13] While I do not have enough expertise to appropriately articulate that reality, I know it to be true from personal experience. The music in an elevator differs from the music in a night club. The music in a restaurant differs from the music at a basketball game. In the same way, the music of a sanctuary differs from that of a concert hall. The stylistic power of music prohibits certain styles of music from finding their way into the sanctuary for corporate worship. Some styles of Christian music may be appropriate for a concert hall or outdoor rock festival or an infant nursery, but fail to provide adequate support for congregational song or fail to create the kind of atmosphere that encourages the worship of a loving and majestic God. Liturgical music is meant to be a

> polished silver chalice, in which the strong wine of God's love is given to the rest of us.... What matters is that in worship we should enter the presence of the living God. And the music, if it is appropriate, can be a vital element in that awesome event.[14]

With that realization, those planning worship should implement styles of music that, when combined with truthful lyrics, draw hearts and minds together while enabling us to worship our Triune God in spirit and in truth. Towards that lofty goal, each congregation must determine the instrumentation that will accompany its worship. This is a local decision determined by specific exigencies of the congregation. Some congregations don't have many options. They worship in the hills of Honduras, without the aid of electricity. Their congregations include one person who owns and plays an acoustic guitar. Like many large suburban congregations, God has blessed my congregation with many musicians, forcing us to make decisions about the instruments that will support congregational song. If we so desire, we could worship accompanied by a pipe organ, a grand piano, a small orchestra, an acoustic guitar, a "rock 'n roll" style band, or by any combination of the above.

---

[13] Michael Horton, *Rediscovering the Drama of Christ-Centered Worship*, 163-187.
[14] N.T. Wright, *For All God's Worth*, 73.

The point to remember is this: it doesn't make a difference. While my Campbellite friends will strongly disagree, I find no biblical directives that define or restrict instrumentation in worship. While style is not neutral, instrumentation for worship is preferential and circumstantial. As a result, my congregation has taken a smorgasbord approach to instrumentation. While the pipe organ is our primary instrument, we utilize a bunch of other instruments including, but not limited to, electronic keyboards and guitars, trumpets and drums. In the process, we have discovered that stringed instruments (acoustic guitars, violin, and piano) have been most effective in uniting four generations of Christians in worship, that the practice of using multiple instruments reflects and affirms the diversity of musical gifts and tastes in the congregation, and that such usage allows for a creative mixture of old and new by which we make music together "for the enjoyment and edification of each other and for the greater glory of God."[15]

Our current practice, however, challenges us as a people. It seems no matter how sanctified, we tend to approach worship as a consumer, expecting our needs to be met. We often struggle, even for a few minutes while seated in a sanctuary, to sacrifice personal preferences out of love for those of others. For that reason, "experts" have determined that a "blended" approach to instrumentation is futile. They believe that different musical tastes and preferences represent a human limitation that we will never transcend in this lifetime. Maybe they are right. I really don't know. I do know that the question of instrumentation should be answered principally, not in response to the self-centered tendencies of saints. It should be answered, minimally, on the basis of the musical gifts God has given a particular community, and on the musical tastes of a diverse, yet covenanted community.

---

[15] Frank Birch Brown, *Good Taste, Bad Taste, and Christian Taste*, 167.

Chapter Six
The Context for Worship

Principle #22 On the Culture of Worship:
Worship is in the world, but not of it.

"Love the Lord your God with all your heart, with all your soul, and with all your mind. This is the first and greatest commandment."
(Matthew 22:37-38)

I was raised in Chicago, but attended college in Nashville, Tennessee. Once on campus, I faced my first "in the world, but not of it" experience. It took place during freshman orientation when a group of fellow students spoke. At that point, I felt like a fish out of water, barely able to understand my classmates who, in turn, got quite a kick out of my "Chicago" accent. Four months after my southern exposure, I went home for Christmas, only to discover, according to my family, that I had picked up a little "drawl." I also picked up a little southern "grace," which my father loved, since I starting responding to his questions with "Yes, sir!" and "No, sir!"

That simple experience illustrates a basic truth: environment affects us in one way or another. It even affects the way we worship. Every Christian community worships in the world and every Christian liturgy is shaped in some measure by the culture of the world. We may even assume that "all liturgical action is culturally conditioned" and that "we cannot escape culture."[1] Carl F.H. Henry writes,

> Every human being is born into some cultural context. None of us can choose, moreover, into which cultural setting he or she will emerge to life on earth. Inevitably a cultural given impinges on us. We learn a particular language in a particular historical age. If we move to another country, a different context of humanly shared believes, ideals, and institutions awaits us. Nobody lives in a cultural vacuum except as exiles sealed off from society.[2]

Scripture addresses that reality with this principle: worship is in the world, but not of it. Our liturgy is in the world; it adapts to the community and culture of the worshipers. The sixteenth century Reformers affirmed this principle by insisting that worship be in the vernacular of a given people. Today, this principle means that those who gather outside a small home in the mountains of Honduras speak Spanish, worship in everyday clothes, with acoustic guitars (since there is no electricity), and learn songs by repetition (since most do not read). Those who drive their cars to worship in a middle-to-upper income suburb in the United States, dress upscale, speak English, employ electronic technology, read bulletins, and sit in a "sacred" space called a "sanctuary."

Every corporate worship experience reflects, to one degree or another, its culture. And that is desirable. Too much of a disconnect between a person's culture and that same person's liturgy creates insurmountable hurdles. Cultural adaptation "keeps worshipers from stumbling over unnecessary obstacles, and helps them engage God more directly." Plus, culturally enriched worship "reflects the glory of God and displays the very complexion of God's creation."[3] The variety of corporate liturgical expressions reflects the rich diversity of our Triune God.

---

[1] John Witvliet, *Worship Seeking Understanding: Windows Into Christian Practice* (Grand Rapids, MI: Baker Book House, 2003), 119.
[2] Carl H.H. Henry, *Twilight of a Great Civilization: The Drift Toward Neo-Paganism* (Westchester, IL: Crossway Books, 1988), 115.
[3] Cornelius Plantinga, Jr. and Sue A. Rozeboom, *Discerning the Spirits: A Guide to Thinking about Christian Worship Today* (Grand Rapids, MI: Eerdmans Publishing Co, 2003), 65, 68.

At the same time, liturgy is not of the world. It does not affirm, implicitly or explicitly, the values of this world. It does not answer the world's questions because they "are not the questions which lead to life."[4] It sustains the unique way of life taught and embodied by Jesus Christ. It conveys the new reality found in Jesus Christ. It encourages worshipers to embrace another way of speaking, of fellowship, and of eating. Consequently, through our liturgy we tell the world that there is "another language and another way of viewing and understanding reality that they should want to learn."[5]

Liturgy is in the world, but not of it. Towards that goal we try to balance the "particularization" of the culture with the "universality" of the Gospel. We accomplish that goal through "theologically informed cultural criticism of our environmental context," an activity prompted by our suspicion that culture accompanies every innovation, in one way or another.[6] Occasionally, we fall to one side or another. We allow culture to influence the liturgy to the point that it is no longer distinctively Christian, or we embrace a liturgy totally disconnected from life. Our goal, however, is an "authentic" liturgy – one that is both faithful to God's revelation and to the situation in which we live.[7]

When, by God's grace, we establish worship patterns that are in the world, but not of it, our liturgy exhibits both continuity and discontinuity with culture. We need not "apologize for ways in which Christian worship is different from the broader culture," or accommodate "cultural pressures to change worship simply because accommodation is easier than resistance to those pressures."[8] We have been called to live as a "radically countercultural and culture-transforming community." We call "people into a new world... that includes new ways of worshiping, singing, and seeing all of life."[9]

---

[4] Leslie Newbigin, *The Gospel in a Pluralistic Society* (Grand Rapids, MI: Eerdmans Publishing Co, 1989), 119.

[5] Robert W. Brimlow, "Solomon's Porch: The Church as Sectarian Ghetto," in *The Church as Counterculture*, edited by Michael L. Budde and Robert W. Brimlow (Albany, NY: State University of New York Press, 2000), 110.

[6] John Witvliet, *Worship Seeking Understanding*, 116.

[7] Lukas Vischer, *Christian Worship in Reformed Churches Past and Present*, 282.

[8] *Authentic Worship in a Changing Culture* (Grand Rapids, MI: CRC Publications, 1997), 61.

[9] *Authentic Worship in a Changing Culture*, 61.

The Context for Worship

Language represents one major application of the "in, but not of," principle. Each local congregation must decide what language it will employ in worship. That decision often provokes tremendous passion, especially among immigrant congregations. Typically, a congregation employs the native tongue of the majority of its worshipers, an exclusive but necessary decision. Some congregations, however, offer separate liturgies for each of the prominent language groups of its people or community.

While the selection of the liturgical "tongue" forces one decision, another still awaits the congregation. Will it employ biblical and theological language in the liturgy, or will it only use the language of the world? Those two options form two poles within which congregations live. On one hand, we don't leave the vocabulary of the world when we gather with Christians for worship. On the other hand, Christians have a dictionary of words that reflect the truths of God's Word and convey the nature of their spiritual experiences. We would expect, then, that the language of the liturgy differ from, to one degree or another, the language of the work place.

While undocumented, I think it safe to state that, in my lifetime, the liturgical language of American Christians has become less biblical and more generic. Spurred, perhaps, by a noble and appropriate desire to be "seeker-sensitive" or to be "real," we have chosen to translate biblical and doctrinal truth into secular language. For years, I supported that trend. However, I have had a change of mind. The turning point for me was when I heard my high-school-dropout father describe his multiple heart surgeries as if he were a surgeon. I still marvel at my father's grasp of his medical condition. He readily and easily discusses each of his twelve pharmaceutical prescriptions. When he gathers with friends who, like him, need boxes to keep all their pills straight, they engage in technical medical dialogue. Their comprehension of medical terms, such as the names of each of their drugs, allows them to discuss their conditions and concerns in great detail. Yet, and here is the tragedy, after over seventy years in the church, my father and I can only engage in elementary theological dialogue.

Why is that? In retrospect, I believe I, as well as others, had made four errors with respect to language. First, I succumbed to intellectual elitism. I assumed that people like my non-educated father couldn't comprehend the deep truths of Scripture. Yet, he proves me wrong when he discusses his heart surgery with physicians and nurses alike. Second, I got sucked into to the trap of substituting psychological language for biblical language. I failed to realize that, while "psychotherapeutic language has helped many people, Christians included, it should be the church's second language; it should not replace the first language of theology."[10] Third, I failed to recognize that the church is, as those outside it expect it to be, a counter-cultural community with a distinctive way of talking, eating, and drinking. As Rodney Clapp notes,

> God is at work, of course, in all of reality, not merely in our fleeting hours of public worship. But humanity is a blinded race, and in worship we have a chance to look on the world as it truly is – the beloved and redeemed creation of God the Father, Son and Holy Spirit.[11]

Fourth, I failed to recognize that by abandoning the language of the Gospel, I helped move the church off of its moorings, thereby letting it float aimlessly into the culture as just another social institution indistinguishable from others.

These days I encourage Christians to remember that, as a covenanted community of believers, congregations have inherited a dictionary filled with words that helps us talk to one another about the truths of this world and of the Gospel. These words, like "regeneration" or "Trinity," summarize great experiential and biblical truths. They help us understand what the Triune God has been about in the world, in the church, in our lives, and in the world. Most importantly, they help us articulate real answers to real questions by real people. They help us communicate the way, the truth and the life to one another and the world. Robert Brimlow poses this challenge with respect to language:

> The problem that the church ought to be confronting when faced with the Lord's charge to us to witness to the nations is not that of finding a way to translate the gospel so that pagans can understand it in their idiom. That is to fall prey to and transform the gospel into the values of the world when what we should be doing is transforming the world into the Kingdom of God. Rather, our problem as church is to find a way to let the world know that there is another language and another way of viewing and understanding reality that they should want to learn.[12]

---

[10] Rodney Clapp, *A Peculiar People*, 105.
[11] Rodney Clapp, *A Peculiar People*, 112.
[12] Robert W. Brimlow, "Solomon's Porch: The Church as Sectarian Ghetto," 109-110.

Principle #23 On The Day of Worship Christians Worship Each Week

> *"On the first day of the week we came together to break bread."*
> *(Acts 20:7)*

As a child the longest ten to fourteen days in my life began on Christmas Day and concluded the Sunday after New Year's Day. The Ebenezer Christian Reformed Church, of which I was a baptized member, hosted a worship service on Christmas Day, a morning and evening service the Sunday after Christmas, a New Year's Eve service, a New Year's Day service, and a morning and evening service the Sunday after New Year's Day. My faithful parents brought me and my siblings to each one. My faithful pastor led all seven services, plus an occasional wedding or funeral.

Now I look back at those days with admiration for my pastor who worked tirelessly and for the congregation who approached worship with expectation. My grandparents, for example, believed that when God's people gather, God pours out unique blessings that they can't get any where else, that more worship means more of those blessings, and that Christians can transform secular holidays into sacred moments to receive such blessings.

Such is not the case in this day and age when most Evangelical congregations worship every Sunday but do not worship on Christmas Day. They view that holiday as a family day. So, when Christmas falls on Sunday they face a major decision: Shall we host a gathering for the family of God? Most go ahead with Sunday services while expecting below average attendance. If they have three morning services, they offer two; or they combine with another congregation in the community. In the year 2005, however, several Evangelical congregations cancelled Sunday services on December 25. The official line from congregational leaders stated that Christmas is a family day and that Christians could receive sufficient blessing while remaining home.

The un-official line, the implicit message within that decision, confused many congregants with the gift of discernment. First, canceling a service because a congregation expects below-average attendance encourages members to conclude that, in some way, the size of the worshiping body dictates the need for worship. Second, canceling a Sunday Christmas Day service encourages members to believe that the blessings received from fellowship with one's earthly family equal, even surpass those received by fellowship with the family of God. Third, canceling a Sunday Christmas Day service contributes to the secularization of the holiday; it treats Christmas as a civic holiday, wrapped in traditional garb, rather than a Christian holiday, connected to the birth of the Messiah. Fourth, when a congregation cancels services on Sunday, December 25, it undercuts the traditional understanding of Sunday as the Lord's Day.

For centuries, Christians have viewed Sunday as a day of corporate worship. While the first generation of Christians gathered on each and every day, the first day of the week was their day of hope and resurrection.[13] The Scriptures illustrate that, long before Constantine legislated a compulsory day of rest by making Sunday the Christian substitute for the Jewish Sabbath, Christians "had their own day."[14] It was on the first day of the week that our triune God began the process of creation. It was on the first day of the week that God the Father raised Jesus Christ, His Son, from the grave by the power of the Holy Spirit. It was on the first day of the week that the risen Christ appeared to His disciples (John 20:19-26). It was on the first day of the week that the Holy Spirit fell upon the first church in Jerusalem. It was on the first day of the week that the church we know was born. It was on the first day of the week that they gathered for worship (Act 20:7). While a normal day of the week for everyone else, the early Christians transformed Sunday into a day of remembrance and expectation.[15] In summary, Scripture leads modern Christians to conclude that they should gather each week on Sunday, the Lord's Day.

Some Christians deepen their commitment to the Lord's Day by equating it with the Sabbath Day. They believe that "the Sabbath is the day Christians are to set apart for private and public acts of worship; the Lord's Day is the Christian Sabbath."[16] Question 103 of the Heidelberg Catechism asks, "What is God's will for you in the fourth commandment?" The answer:

---

[13] Horace T. Allen, Jr., "Calendar and Lectionary in Reformed Perspective and History," *Christian Worship in Reformed Churches Past and Present*, edited by Lukas Vischer (Grand Rapids, MI: Eerdmans Publishing Co., 2003), 397.
[14] Alexander Schmemann, *For the Life of the World*, 50-52.
[15] See Hughes Oliphant Old, *Worship Reformed According to Scripture*, 23-32.
[16] D.G. Hart and John R. Mueller, *With Reverence and Awe*, 63.

First, that the gospel ministry and education for it be maintained, and that, especially on the festive day of rest, I regularly attend the assembly of God's people to learn what God's Word teaches, to participate in the sacraments, to pray to God publicly, and to bring Christian offerings for the poor.

Second, that every day of my life I rest from my evil ways, let the Lord work in me through his Spirit, and so begin already in this life the eternal Sabbath.

The Westminster Shorter Catechism asks, "How is the Sabbath to be sanctified? The answer:

> The Sabbath is to be sanctified by a holy resting all that day, even from such worldly employments and recreations as are lawful on other days; and spending the whole time in the public and private exercises of God's worship, except so much as is to be taken up in works of necessity and mercy.

Others reject Sunday as the Lord's Day, considering "every day alike" (Romans 14:5-6). Some contemporary evangelical high-tech congregations in America treat Sunday like any day of the week. Since the early Christians met every day, they worship on any day. "Fully convinced in their own minds" that Christ is Lord of all, they don't regard one day as "more special" than another. On that premise, they may change their day of weekly worship to any day of the week. One impetus for this flexibility has been the desire to host evangelistic services for unbelievers on Sunday mornings. Canceling Sunday services on Christmas Day represents the logical outcome of the rejection of Sunday as the Lord's Day.

Personally, I react to the ease with which some modern Christians reject the two thousand year old biblical tradition of the Lord's Day. I don't find their arguments convincing, especially when linked to the whole "seek-sensitive" model of moving the weekly gathering for worship to another day and using the Sunday morning slot for an evangelistic service. As I documented (Principles #18), I believe corporate worship is an evangelistic service.

But I also react to those who equate the Lord's Day with the Sabbath Day. I don't find that equation modeled by the first generation of Jewish

Christians who both recognized the Sabbath Day as a day of rest and gathered with Christians on the Lord's Day. Referring to Sunday as the Sabbath seems more like the fruit of a post-Constantinian world view which, centuries later, received even more prominence within Puritanism. With respect to this issue, this much I am sure of:

1) The rhythm of one day of rest every seven days is a wonderful gift from God and necessary for our well-being,

2) The principle of weekly worship on the Lord's Day rests on a strong biblical tradition,

3) For many Americans, the Sabbath Day and the Lord's Day are the same day, which has been a special blessing for years, and

4) For many others, like pastors, medical professionals, and civil servants, the Lords' Day and the Sabbath Day must be two different days.

Principle #24 On the Form and Freedom of Worship: God delights in both form and freedom.

*"These people honor me with their lips,
but their hearts are far from me." (Matthew 15:8)*

When the people who call themselves the Palos Heights Christian Reformed gather for worship, they humble themselves before the order of worship prescribed by the Elders. So, when the pastor or worship leader asks them to speak, they speak. When invited to stand, they stand until someone asks them to be seated. When encouraged to pray, they pray. Like a well-practiced unit of Marines, they worship in step, not only with words, but with actions. Nearly every aspect of their worship is formed by the liturgy. Worshipers do not perceive permission to vary from the pattern. Uniformity is the norm.

My church away from church is the Apostolic Church of God in Chicago, led by Bishop Arthur Brazier. I love worshiping with this predominantly African American congregation because it grants me freedom to worship in a manner consistent with my personality. When moved by a solo, I can stand, even though no one around me stands. When touched by the sermon, I can affirm the proclaimed word with an audible "Amen." Permission has been given to worship as the "Spirit leads."

The difference between those two worship experiences was accented for me one Christmas season when I had the privilege of worshiping with both congregations. During both services Handel's "Hallelujah Chorus" was played and sung. In Palos Heights, when the first note was struck, the entire congregation stood. In Chicago, when the first note was struck, a handful of people stood. Some measures later, a few more stood. By the end of the piece, about half the congregation was standing, while the other half remained seated. So, in Palos Heights the formed worship experience invited worshipers to humble themselves before the liturgy and follow the traditional pattern of standing for Handel's majestic piece. In Chicago, the free worship experience invited worshipers to stand if they wanted to. Neither approach is wrong, just different.

The discussion between free and formed worship has precedent in seventeenth-century England. The Free Church tradition protested against "formed worship" or the ecclesiastical mandate to use the Book of Common Prayer. Free Church proponents desired freedom to worship according to God's Word. They rejected the use of the Lectionary and clerical vestments, and insisted on the the faithful exposition of the Scriptures, the practice of extemporaneous prayers, congregational singing, and the simple administration of the Lord's Supper. The Free Church tradition has held a prominent place in America for many decades and has formed the foundation of most Evangelical worship in this country. D. Martin Lloyd-Jones, a free worshiper, offers the typical critique of formed worship:

> It is very interesting to notice that as men and women know less and less about a living spiritual experience, the more formal does their worship become... This is because of the low level of spirituality. Conversely, when people come to a living experience of God they rely less and less upon forms.[17]

---

[17] D.M. Lloyd-Jones, *Romans: An Exposition of Chapter 8:5-17 The Sons of God* (Grand Rapids, MI: Zondervan Publishing House, 1975), 242

Proponents of formed worship believe that the utilization of forms allows for greater participation by the congregation, provides for a biblically and theologically rich liturgy, protects the congregation from being conformed to the world, and provides for a more formative liturgical experience. They testify that forms do not negate the potential for a living spiritual experience, and counter that the absence of forms often leads to anything but a spiritual experience. In their estimation, many free worship services become polluted with meaningless jabber which fails to stir the hearts and minds of God's people.

Proponents of free worship counter by highlighting the inherent weaknesses of formed worship. First, it provides the structure for worshipers to honor God with their lips but not, necessarily, with their hearts. In other words, form worshipers may come to the sanctuary and go through the motions without really worshiping the Lord. Of course, that could be said of any service – formed or free. Second, as Donald Bloesch notes, formed worship may convert the liturgy "into prescribed rituals and formulas, thereby blocking the free movement of the Spirit in the congregation."[18]

The congregation I serve has adopted a "semi-formed" approach to worship, one consistent with its heritage as a Dutch Reformed fellowship, and one responsive to our culture in Chicago, where Moody Bible Institute, the citadel of Fundamentalism, has exercised tremendous influence through its radio station. On the "Free" church side, we insist upon expositional preaching, congregational singing, and the simple service of the sacraments. In addition, we haven't been convinced of the need to follow the lectionary or wear clerical vestments. On the "Formed" church side, we utilize unison readings and prayers, the Lord's Prayer and the Apostles' Creed, as well as responsive readings: all as tools to involve the congregation in nearly every facet of the service. Plus, we have discovered, perhaps accidentally, that formed worship allows more members to participate in the liturgy, including children, mentally impaired adults, and, when memorized, the sight impaired. By adopting this middle road, we believe we allow for the free movement of the Spirit without abandoning structure.[19] We also affirm that since "God delights in both form and freedom, there is value

---

[18] Donald Bloesch, *The Church: Sacraments, Worship, Ministry, Mission* 36.
[19] Donald Bloesch, *The Church: Sacraments, Worship, Ministry, Mission*, 142-143.

both in the freely charismatic and in the regular activities of the Spirit in the ordered community."[20]

Principle #25 On the Space for Worship: God's people can worship anywhere.

> *"For where two or three come together in my name, there am I with them." (Matthew 18:20)*

I have never "planted" a congregation but I know it is tough work. You start with a congregation of one or more individuals (depending on the size of your family). You move into a community, rent space in an office complex, market your ministry to your neighbors, gather small groups in your living room for Bible studies and, after a lengthy period of time, invite people to gather for corporate worship in rented space.

One benefit of being a church planter is that you don't have to deal with the way things have always been done. You start with a clean slate. You determine, for example, the space for corporate worship, often renting generic auditoriums without religious symbols. Established congregations made that decision years, if not decades ago. Since that time they have, intentionally or unintentionally, affirmed their decision on space up to the present day.

It is a good exercise, however, to ask whether the gathering space for worship should be sacred (that is, set apart) or common. Scripture illustrates the poles of that decision. The first Christians gathered in common space, such as the homes of believers. The church before Christ worshiped in sacred or set apart space. What shall we do?

Before we answer that question we should acknowledge that it only has validity because God has provided us, as American Christians, with sufficient financial resources to worship anywhere. My congregation, for example, could worship in a pole barn or a multi-million dollar sanctuary. So, a better question might be, "How shall we disburse God's money?" While people can gather for worship anywhere, my congregation has

---

[20] Clark Pinnock, *Flame of Love: A Theology of the Holy Spirit* (Downers Grove, IL: InterVarsity Press, 1996), 131.

chosen, with countless congregations throughout history, to worship in space consecrated for worship. In so doing, they acknowledge that space can "elevate the human spirit," "speak of what cannot be fully understood," and remind us of a "holiness beyond words."[21]

Some may argue that Christians should worship in common space, such as a multi-purpose room and, then, dedicate more money for ministry and missions. I find that argument unconvincing for one simple reason: it assumes that God's resources are limited to what we can touch and see. God, the creator, can do far more than we imagine, and His resources are not scarce. If the Lord wants a community to worship in sacred space, He will provide the resources to construct that space. If not, the community will worship in a gym or someone's home. A. Daniel Frankforter offers this balanced response:

> The sincerity of a congregation's piety is proportional not to the cost of the sanctuary it raises, but to the sacrifice the building represents. There are lavish temples that do no nothing but serve rich egos, and there are simple churches that are priceless offerings – the equivalent of the widow's mite.[22]

The congregation that opts for sacred space will give special attention to the broader subject of architecture and the narrower subject of furnishings. Authors Donald Bruggink and Carl Droppers begin their unparalleled work, *Christ and Architecture,*" with these words:

> Architecture for churches is a matter of gospel. A church that is interested in proclaiming the gospel must also be interested in architecture, for year after year the architecture of the church proclaims a message that either augments the preached Word or conflicts with it.[23]

---

[21] Howard L. Rice and James C. Huffstutler, *Reformed Worship*, 131.
[22] A. Daniel Frankforter, *Stones for Bread* (Grand Rapids, MI: Zondervan Publishing Co, 1995), 158-159.
[23] Donald J. Bruggink and Carl H. Droppers, *Christ and Architecture: Building Presbyterian/Reformed Churches* (Grand Rapids, MI: Eerdmans Publishing Company, 1965), 1.

Bruggink and Droppers validate their thesis with both a reference to God's detailed concern about the construction of the tabernacle and the temple, and with an illustration from the sixteenth-century Reformation:

> The inherited Roman Catholic churches were not changed because of aesthetic inclinations on the part of the Reformed clergy, or because of a new stylistic fad. They were changed because the gospel was so important that the Reformers could not allow the churches to remain as they were. The Reformers were acutely conscious of the power of architecture and the constant message that it held for the people.[24]

Each congregation must wrestle with the implications of its theology for its worship space. The space within which we worship says something about our view of worship and the one we worship. As a lifelong Chicagoan, I remain amazed by the plethora of magnificent sanctuaries constructed by poor immigrant communities. My amazement deepens when I compare those edifices to the sacred space constructed by the grandchildren of those immigrants. Today's American Evangelical church seems much more interested in building second homes and driving luxury vehicles than sacrificing such pleasures for the construction of worship space that stirs the heart. Consequently, they construct standardized, multipurpose structures, decorated, like a Christmas tree, with churchy ornaments. Of course, it is not all about money. A. Daniel Frankforter writes,

> To be consecrated by and for worship a building need not be elaborate, but it must have integrity. It must proclaim its people's belief that what they do within it is important enough to deserve the best they can provide. That may mean soaring vaults and gold chalices or log cabins and clay cups. What is important is not the value, but the commitment to honor God.[25]

Each congregation must wrestle with the implications of its theology for its furnishings. As a Reformed congregation, for example, we believe the preaching of the Word is the center piece of the liturgy. As a result, the

---

[24] Donald J. Bruggink and Carl H. Droppers, *Christ and Architecture*, 2-3.
[25] A. Daniel Frankforter, *Stones for Bread*, 159.

pulpit is front and center, with the pews facing the pulpit. We also believe that individuals enter the church through baptism. This means that the baptismal could properly be placed at the entrance to the sanctuary, but we place it at the front of the sanctuary so the congregation can witness the individuals received into its fellowship. We have a table alongside the pulpit that we refer to as the "Lord's Table," from which we serve the Lord's Supper. It is called a table, not an altar. We have good acoustics that amplify and thereby, encourage our congregational singing, a hallmark of our tradition. We have but one religious symbol in the sanctuary, a cross etched in a stained glass window.

Not all our space makes theological sense. Our choir loft is behind the pulpit. Several Reformed congregations place their choir loft in the balcony or in the back of the sanctuary, accenting its supportive role and diminishing the temptation of performance. Our pews don't have kneelers. It seems our fore-parents cut them out, along with every vestige of the Virgin Mary, thinking that they were both essentially "Roman." I wish we had kneelers. Then we could really "kneel before the Lord our Maker." The 75 foot length of our sanctuary, with two sections of twenty pews each, is not as effective for communication between speaker and listener as a shorter and wider fan-shaped sanctuary. Worshipers confined to wheelchairs must sit in the back or front because the sanctuary floor is sloped. The "Lord's Table" is not like the tables we find in our homes. When placed against a wall, it looks more like an altar upon which one makes a sacrifice (or a place for a large floral arrangement leftover from someone's funeral), than the table upon which Christ shared the Passover feast with the Apostles. We would be better served by a rugged, wooden table with legs, surrounded by a couple chairs, and a rudimentary table setting or two. Finally, our cross is too pretty and fails to convey the passion of Christ for our sins.

Our congregation is not alone. Consistency between sacred space and theology poses a challenge for many congregations. Inherited space forms another. So many congregations own antiquated buildings that hinder, rather than enhance their worship ministries. Many sanctuaries, for example, limit accessibility to the able-bodied, provide minimal space for instrumentalists, have poor sight lines and lighting, and fail to reflect the beauty and grandeur of God. Congregations with such restrictions may want to consider modifying their sacred space or, if the Lord provides the funds, constructing new space. Usually, however, congregants cherish the space within which they have shared countless memories of God's grace. So they resist any attempts for change or modification. It is then that space becomes an idol, though few recognize it as such.

Principle #26 On the Aesthetics of Worship: We worship in beauty, without idols.

You shall not make for yourself an idol in the form of anything in heaven above or on the earth beneath or in the waters below. You shall not bow down to them or worship them; for I, the LORD your God, am a jealous God, punishing the children for the sin of the fathers to the third and fourth generation of those who hate me, but showing love to a thousand generations of those who love me and keep my commandments. (Exodus 20:4-6)

Reformed Christians have a long tradition of minimizing the role of the visual arts. Traditionally, we have taken seriously the Old Testament prohibition of visual representations of God. The Heidelberg Catechism clearly articulates our perspective:

> What is God's will for us in the second commandment? That we in no way make any image of God nor worship him in any other way than he has commanded in his Word.
>
> May we then not make any image at all? God can not and may not be visibly portrayed in any way. Although creatures may be portrayed, yet God forbids making or having such images if one's intention is to worship them or to serve God through them!
>
> But may not images be permitted in the churches as teaching aids for the unlearned? No, we shouldn't try to be wiser than God. He wants his people instructed by the living preaching of his Word – not by idols that cannot even talk.[26]

---

[26] Lord's Day 35.

Following that teaching, many Reformed Christians do not allow visual representations of God in their worship spaces, fearing that they may lead worshipers, prone to idolatry, to transfer trust from one to the other.[27]

Interestingly, some Reformed communities allow for visual representations of God in their sanctuaries. The worship center of the First Reformed Church of Berwyn, Illinois, for example, includes two beautiful stained-glass windows. One portrays the ascension of Christ, while the other portrays Christ as the shepherd of the sheep. While worshiping in that space I have been emotionally moved by those portraits, yet wonder how they made it into the sanctuary. The catechism of the congregation is unequivocal on the subject. My hunch is that they made it in because the congregation's experience led them to disagree with the conclusions of the two young men who wrote the Heidelberg Catechism. They believe that the portraits of Christ enhance their worship.

While some Reformed Christians stand on their confessions and prohibit portraits or icons of God in their sanctuaries, and while many more simply ignore their confessions and do whatever they like, I suggest a third alternative. Let contemporary Reformed Christians revisit and reform the traditional prohibition of visual portraits of God in the sanctuary. If we take this option, we may conclude that the Reformers, influenced by their own package of issues, over-reacted in their prohibition of visual portraits of God in the sanctuary. If we allow for that possibility, we receive permission to craft a new confession for Reformed Christians who take seriously the potential for art to hinder and help the corporate worship of the faithful. Such a document would open the door for congregations to call and empower gifted artists, so that they may employ their God-given gifts in a way that enriches the worship of the gathered community.

Minimally, a new confessional statement would articulate and affirm the following principles. First, God created a world characterized by beauty that exerts power on people. In Genesis 2:9 we read that "the Lord God made all kinds of trees to grow out of the ground – trees that were pleasing to the eye and good for food." In Genesis 3:6, we read the "woman saw that the fruit of the tree was good for food and pleasing to the eye." William Dyrness writes "the world seems to be shaped in such

---

[27] Elsie Ann McKee, "Reformed Worship in the Sixteenth Century," 13.

a way that it welcomes our appreciation of its beauty."[28] He points the reader to the work of Elaine Scarry who believes that the "moment one comes into the presence of something beautiful it greets you."[29] Dyrness, then, offers this commentary:

> Something of the loving goodness of God shines through our experience of beauty. This is why we are inevitably moved to put ourselves in the way of such experiences. We deeply long not only for such beauty but, Christians believe, for relationship with the personal presence lying beneath such beauty. As a result, the experience of great beauty often moves unbelievers to seek God, just as it often moves believers to praise, even to sing or dance.[30]

Second, God has gifted some of his children with the ability to create beautiful visual art. In other words, as John Calvin taught, the Holy Spirit is the source of genuine artistic creativity.[31] The "true artist," then, is "someone whose creativity is a painful yet joyful response to God's providence and grace."[32] As a church called to affirm the gifts of God among his people, we must provide freedom for gifted artists to minister to the church and community in the name of Jesus. This ministry may entail art that finds its way into the sanctuary because of the "depth of its human expression or because of the sense of transcendence that its beauty generates."[33] Or it may find a home in a downtown gallery or an emerging gallery on the campus of a congregation.

Third, the Holy Spirit may employ art as a tool for spiritual growth and development. John de Gruchy writes,

---

[28] William A. Dyrness, *Visual Faith: Art, Theology, and Worship in Dialogue* (Grand Rapids, MI: Baker Book House, 2001), 141.
[29] Elaine Scarry, *On Beauty and Being Just* (Princeton University Press, 1999), 25-26.
[30] Dyrness, *Visual Faith: Art, Theology, and Worship in Dialogue*, 142.
[31] John Calvin, *Institutes of the Christian Religion* II.2.15-16.
[32] John W. de Gruchy, "Holy Beauty: A Reformed Perspective on Aesthetics within a World of Ugly Injustice," *Reformed Theology for the Third Christian Millennium*, edited by B.A. Gerrish (Westminster John Knox Press, 2003), 13-25.
[33] Frank Burch Brown, *Good Taste, Bad Taste, and Christian Taste*, 55.

> Art enhances faith, but is not a replacement for faith. Art provides a vehicle for the Spirit, but is not the power of the Spirit…. Great art speaks to the soul… (It) helps us perceive reality in a new way, and by so doing, it opens up possibilities of transformation.

As I typed that last quotation, "Rick" dropped in to see me. He worshiped with us last Sunday and picked up on my preaching schedule for Advent, which included a sermon on Joseph (Matthew 1:18-25). He dropped off a post-card sized copy of an artist's rendering of Joseph, Mary and the infant Jesus in a barn on that first Christmas. In the portrait, Joseph holds Jesus while Mary sleeps. While most people might describe the piece as "kitsch," he loves it because it shows him a side of Joseph he had not thought about: a devout man assuming his responsibility as the earthly father of someone else's child. Rick's experience, shared by many others in different ways, illustrates how art enhances faith and speak to our souls.

Fourth, God expects excellence and truth in all aspects of worship, including art. Without responsible oversight, however, ecclesiastical art may, as de Gruchy notes, degenerate into an uncritical ecclesial kitsch or conform to the dictates of "high culture." In both options art loses its "theological integrity and coherence."[34] To affirm artists and free them for ministry in church and community, a congregation would be advised to develop guidelines applied by advisors with knowledge of both art and the congregation's confessions. Without such, sanctuaries quickly take on the appearance of a craft show in a local gymnasium, with a little bit of this and a little bit of that, but without a common thread connecting them all together. While politically difficult, congregations that succeed in this area will find ways to say "no" to certain forms of art while joyously affirming art as a gift from God.

---

[34] John W. de Gruchy, "Holy Beauty," 13-25.

Principle #27 On the Technology of Worship: Worship relies on technology.

"God blessed them and said to them, 'Be fruitful and increase in number; fill the earth and subdue it. Rule over the fish of the sea and the birds of the air and over every living creature that moves on the ground.'" (Genesis 1:28)

No question about it – my favorite teachers were those who provided outlines or manuscripts of their lectures. Those tools eased my load in the classroom. I didn't have to work so hard at listening to the emphases and development of my instructor's essay. Matter of fact, I could pretty much daydream through most of the presentation. Today, I am willing to wager that my instructors believed that the mass production of their lectures in manuscript or outline form was a beneficial use of technology. Now, I can see that, while it had some value, it also encouraged laziness for this listener.

That little vignette from my past leads me to wonder about the benefits of technology for the worshiper. Should I provide a written outline of my sermon or flash bullet points from my message on a screen. Initially, it seems innocent enough, and even helpful, but is it? What does the Bible have to say about the relationship between technology and worship?

Ironically, the biblical foundation for understanding the relationship between technology and worship is a place without technology, the Garden of Eden. In Genesis 1:26 we read these words of God, "Let us make man in our image, in our likeness, and let them rule over the fish of the sea and the birds of the air, over the livestock, over all the earth, and over all the creatures that move along the ground." Al Wolters is one of many who refers to that verse as the cultural or creation mandate. Commenting on its significance, he writes,

> The creation mandate provides a sort of climax to the six days of creation. The stage with all its rich variety of props has been set by the stage director, the actors are introduced, and as the curtain rises and the stage director moves backstage, they are given their opening cue. The drama

of human history is about to begin, and the first and foundational Word of God to his children is the command to "fill and subdue."[35]

As we move to the second chapter of Genesis, we find God creating Adam from the earth and placing "him in the Garden of Eden to work it and take care of it" (:15). The Lord then creates Eve, first as Adam's companion and, then, as his co-worker. Together, as the first married couple, Adam and Eve "represent the beginnings of societal life; their task of tending the garden, the primary task of agriculture, represents the beginnings of cultural life."[36]

Like Adam and Eve, we tend God's creation. We "participate in the ongoing creational work of God." We are "God's helpers in executing to the end the blueprint for his masterpiece." We do so with optimism relishing the opportunity to bring "to fruition the possibilities of development implicit in the work of God's hands." We recognize, with Al Wolters, that the created order includes the potential for the development of great marvel, as well as "positive possibilities for service to God in such areas as politics and the film arts, computer technology and business administration, developmental economics and skydiving." [37]

The creation mandate, then, provides the foundation upon which we appropriate technology in worship. No one has developed the connection between the two better than Quentin Schultze, Professor of Communication Arts and Science at Calvin College in Grand Rapids, Michigan. In his book "High Tech Worship," he offers several tools for contemporary Christians seeking to articulate the appropriate relationship between technology and worship. First, he provides a useful description of technology. In his estimation, technology includes: (1) the physical devices or tools that we use to develop God's creation, (2) the meanings that we attach to these devices, and (3) the ways that we use them.[38] We may flesh out Schultze's threefold description through application. One technology

---

[35] Albert M. Wolters, *Creation Regained: Biblical Basics for a Reformational Worldview* (Grand Rapids, MI: Eerdmans Publishing Co, 1985), 37-38.

[36] Albert M. Wolters, *Creation Regained*.

[37] Albert M. Wolters, *Creation Regained*.

[38] Quentin J. Schultze, *High-Tech Worship: Using Presentational Technologies Wisely* (Grand Rapids, Bake Book Houses, 2004), 43.

at the heart of the sixteenth-century Reformation, for example, was the printing press (a tool), that led to the mass production of the Bible (its use), so that Christians could read the Bible in their native tongue (its value). One of the more popular technologies in modern worship, to cite another example, is an amplification system, a tool that magnifies the preacher's voice (its use) so that Christians can hear the sermon (its value).

Second, Schultze reminds us that "worship always relies on human skills and techniques, if not particular technologies." Looking over the history of the Church, we discover that "worshipers have long fashioned raw materials into such worship artifacts as chalices, stained glass, candles, incense, and crosses."[39] The questions we face today, then, are not new. God's children have perpetually wrestled with discerning the proper relationship between worship and technology. Sometimes our technology led to marvelous results for worship, such as the printing press or an amplification system. At other times we blundered, as in the creation of golden calves.

Third, Schultze asserts that "communication technologies are not neutral tools that merely carry intended messages." The internet, electronic mail, power point presentations, video projectors, and the like "connote power, efficiency, and control." In other words, technology appears "slick," which is to say that everything fits, everything works together, everything is in place, like a Broadway play or Hollywood movie. The problem with slick worship is that the world is not slick and we are not slick. Do we really want to create an atmosphere where everything works and fits together for a gathering of broken saints who have gathered, with all of their shortcoming and sins, for grace and peace in the name of Jesus?

Albert Borgmann echoes Schultze's assertion that technologies carry messages. In his work, *Power Failure: Christianity in the Culture of Technology*, Borgmann establishes this about technology: it is a device that makes life easier. Technology makes something available to us in a comfortable manner. Today, for example, scholars may complete a significant percentage of their research without ever stepping into a library. Shoppers may purchase gifts, groceries and garments without ever leaving their homes. Surely, technology makes life easier, but it is not value-neutral. When asked if technology is just a tool, Borgmann forcefully responds,

---

[39] Quentin J. Schultze, *High-Tech Worship*, 17.

No. It's an inducement, and it's so strong that for the most part people find themselves unable to refuse it. To proclaim it to be a neutral tool flies in the face of how people behave. Why do 90 percent of all families or households watch television after dinner? Is it because they decided that that's the best way to spend their time? No, something else must be going on. And what's going on is that the culture around us--including work that is draining, food that's easily available, and television shows made as attractive as some of the best minds in our country can make them encourages us to plop down in front of the TV and spend two hours there.[40]

Fourth, Schultze reminds us to view technology as a means to an end, not an end in itself. He encourages us to "begin with God's intrinsic designs for worship rather than with a mere human desire for technological efficiency and control – as if we could socially engineer perfect worship on our own without God."[41] Perhaps you have experienced what appeared to be a nonsensical use of technology in worship. Recently, I worshiped with a congregation that has sung out of a hymn book for nearly fifty years and that has hymn books in their pews. I was quite surprised, then, when the hymn books remained in the racks while we sang from words projected on a screen. I still don't understand the purpose for that use of technology by that congregation? In retrospect, it seems to have served but one purpose: it made worship easier for those who didn't want to be bothered by opening a book.

Fifth, Schultze provides a balanced perspective about the use of technology in worship. He reminds us that its use is not either-or; it is "Yes, but."

> Yes, we will consider using it to service our neighbors as ourselves, but we will not be duped by inflated rhetoric about its inherent goodness or badness. Yes, new technologies are part of the unfolding of God's original creation, but we fallen human beings will never be able to use them to usher in heaven on earth. The yes is our faith in God to bless

---

[40] David Wood, "Prime Time: Albert Borgmann on Taming Technology," *Christian Century* 120 (August 23, 2003).
[41] Schultze, *High-Tech Worship*, 23.

our imperfect use of technology; the but is our admission of foolishness and hubris – all sin.[42]

As Christians, then, seeking to fulfill the creation mandate, we resist the temptation to suppose that "any technological innovation has a one-sided effect." We realize, as Neil Postman writes, that "every technology is both a burden and a blessing; not either-or, but this-and-that."[43] Consequently, we don't adopt technology but adapt it to serve our specific purposes for the congregation-specific worship of God.

---

[42] Schultze, *High-Tech Worship*, 43.
[43] Neil Postman, *Technopoly: The Surrender of Culture to Technology* (New York, NY: Vantage Books, 1992), 4-5.

Conclusion

**Principle #28 On Daily Worship:
We worship every day.**

> *"In view of God's mercy, offer your bodies as living sacrifices, holy and pleasing to God – this is your spiritual act of worship." (Romans 12:1)*

Each week we have an opportunity to gather with our Christian community and worship the Lord, to join our voices in song and praise to the Lord, to declare the worthiness of the Lord with our prayers of adoration, both spoken and sung, and to receive a Word from the Lord. Worship, however, is not a once-a-week experience. When we leave the gathered community to disburse throughout the world, we may, then, worship the Lord by offering our "bodies as living sacrifices to the Lord, holy and pleasing to God, as our spiritual act of worship." In other words, worship may be "our very way of day-to-day life."[1] Commentating on Romans 12:1, Douglas Moo wrote,

> Worship is the way we live, not what we do on Sunday morning. We worship God by giving ourselves in sacrificial service to

---

[1] Robert E. Webber, *Worship is a Verb: Eight Principles for Transforming Worship* (Peabody, MA: Hendrickson Publishers, 1992), 204.

our Lord. We are to serve him every day, every hour, and every minute.[2]

John Stott concurs:

> We worship God by giving ourselves in sacrificial service to our Lord. We are to serve him every day, every hour, and every minute... All of our life is to be a continuous worship of the God who created and redeemed us.[3]

What is the relationship between Sunday and Monday? While we don't want to fall into the trap of viewing worship as a means to an end or as a "re-fueling station" in life, we must acknowledge that our Sunday gathering prompts Monday worship, "not just with our mouths, but with our whole beings."[4] In the best case scenario, our Sunday liturgy pushes us back to our homes and into the market place where we may offer our everyday, ordinary lives to the Lord as an offering. Hopefully, the impetus for this movement from the sanctuary to the world comes, not from a spirit of obligation or guilt, but, from a spirit of gratitude born out of God's grace. Like those who first witnessed the resurrection, we hope our encounter with Christ in worship motivates us to run to the world as instruments of God's redeeming grace. As we leave the sanctuary each Sunday, might we say with Paul,

> I have been crucified with Christ and I no longer live, but Christ lives in me. The life I live in the body, I live by faith in the Son of God who loved me and gave himself for me (Galatians 2:20).

If we fail to do so, Nicholas Wolterstorff writes, "a shadow is cast over the worship, and its authenticity is brought into question."[5] Don Saliers even

---

[2] Douglas J. Moo, *Romans* (Grand Rapids, MI: Zondervan Publishing Co., 2000), 397.
[3] John Stott, *Romans: God's Good News for the World* (Downers Grove, IL: InterVarsity Press, 1994), 320-324.
[4] Marva Dawn, *The Hilarity of Community; Romans 12 and How to Be the Church* (Grand Rapids, MI:L Eerdmans Publishing Co., 1992), 12.
[5] Nicolas Wolterstorff, *Until Justice and Peace Embrace* (Grand Rapids, MI: Eerdmans Publishing Co., 1983), 156-157.

suggests that the liturgy remains incomplete until the worship of God leads to works of justice and mercy in the world.[6] Echoing Wolterstorff and Saliers, Lukas Vischer writes that the credibility of a worship experience depends on the "willingness of the community to share in God's movement of love to the world."[7]

If those scholars speak truth, as I believe they do, American Christians are in trouble. On one hand, national polls claim that as many as fifty million Christians live in the United States of America, and that a large percentage of Americans gather each week for corporate worship. On the other hand, observers outside of the USA, and many citizens within it, describe American culture as increasingly secular. How can there be such a disconnect between worship and life? How can so many people be "going to church" on Sunday and our culture fail to show evidence of transformation by the Gospel? Can we come to any other conclusion than that the professed faith and worship of a large number of Americans has little impact upon the culture in which they live?

Some may suggest that the culprit here is not our worship, but the post-modern premise that public truth, the world of facts, differs from private truth, the world of opinions, i.e., faith. Today, most people appear to believe that a person's religious convictions are a private matter and that they have few implications for society. On Sunday, a politician, for example, may privately oppose abortion on demand, but come Monday, he or she will publicly support it – and have no difficulty justifying his or her different positions.

That view of truth, which some lament as the "privatization of faith," seems to have quietly slipped into the consciousness of American Christians who view corporate worship as an end in itself, with little connection to the world. Consequently, they "go to church" to "get something out of it" for themselves. They participate in the activities of the gathered community to nourish their souls, fuel their faith, or escape the problems of the world. However, their worship doesn't influence their lives in the world.

---

[6]Don Saliers, "Liturgy and Ethics: Some New Beginnings," in *Liturgy and the Moral Self*, edited by E Byron Anderson and Bruce T. Morrill (Collegeville: MN, The Liturgical Press, 1998.), 25.
[7]Lukas Vischer, *Christian Worship in Reformed Churches Past and Present*, 415.

Conclusion

If we affirmed a "Christ versus Culture" model of relating to the world, that situation would not be so problematic. Most Christians, however, believe that God has called us to be the salt and light of the world, to extend the reign of Christ over every nook and cranny of the earth. We believe that God has called us to "go into every sector of public life to claim it for Christ, to unmask the illusions which have remained hidden, and to expose all areas of public life to the illumination of the Gospel."[8] We believe, following the lead of the apostle Paul, that God has called us to transform the world. So, we must insist that those who gather for worship on Sunday depart from that gathering intent on serving Christ in the world.

That explains the significance of the final movement of the liturgy. When nearly all has been said and done, the final movement commissions the gathered community to service beyond the walls of the sanctuary. Through scripture and song, the worshipers should be sent back into the world as witnesses of the Gospel and as servants of Christ. As they leave the sanctuary, the liturgy reminds each of God's people that they are about to re-enter the world, hoping to "make things right."[9] Craig Dykstra writes:

> We are sent by Christ into whatever betrays God's purposes and love – wherever that might be. And we are sent not to bring a message of our own but to be the sent people of God there, to be signs of the presence of God there.[10]

Within such a context, the "Benediction," or closing words, takes on more significance. Personally, when I offer my closing words to the congregation, I feel like a commander sending his troops to battle, unsure who will return the following week, or like a school administrator sending out his or her graduates to find their place in the world, realizing some

---

[8] Leslie Newbigin, *The Gospel in a Pluralistic Society*, 232-233.
[9] Walter J. Burghardt's definition of justice may be found in his "Worship and Justice Reunited," in *Liturgy and Justice: To Worship God in Spirit and Truth*, Anne Y. Koester, editor (Collegeville, MN: The Liturgical Press, 2002.
[10] Craig Dykstra, *Growing in the Life of Faith: Education and Christian Practices* (Louisville, KY: Geneva Press, 1999), 159.

may get confused and lost along the way, or like a parent dropping a child off for his or her first day at school. I have discovered that because we re-enter the world, we long for the love of God the Father, the grace of God the Son, and the communion of the Holy Spirit. It is because we enter un-chartered waters, living in faithful and, often, solitary obedience to God's call, that we hope that the Lord will always turn his face towards us and grant us peace.

Having received such hope, we leave the sanctuary singing with our brothers and sisters in Christ, singing as we re-enter the spiritual battlefield, singing words that encourage our troubled hearts, singing melodies that lighten our loads, singing until we meet again, which, for some of us may not be till Christ returns.

Principle #29 On the Future of Worship: Our worship grants a foretaste of heaven.

> *"You are worthy, our Lord and God, to receive glory and honor and power, for you created all things, and by your will they were created and have their being." (Revelation 4:11)*

The Apocalypse of John was not written for Christians enjoying a vacation aboard a luxurious cruise ship, but for believers experiencing suffering and tribulation.[11] It was written for Christians unsure that God reigned supreme over the world; its visions were meant to strengthen those believers while they suffered persecution from the hands of Rome. The fourth and fifth chapters, for example, encourage perplexed believers with a beautiful vision of their sovereign God. They were to conclude from the vision of the Lamb of God, sitting in the center of the heavenly throne, surrounded by four living creatures and twenty-four elders, that, no matter what they endured on the earth, their Lord reigns in majesty. In the midst of tribulation, they may gaze upon the One who is King of kings and Lord of lords.

That beautiful vision portrays worship by the Church Triumphant. In it we find God the Father sitting on His heavenly throne. John compares

---

[11] See "Idealism," by Sam Hamstra, Jr. *in Four Views of the Book of Revelation*, edited by C. Marvin Pate (Grand Rapids, MI: Zondervan Publishing, Co, 2001).

Conclusion

His appearance to jasper and carnelian, two precious and radiant jewels (4:3). A large and diverse congregation worships the Father, a group that includes four striking creatures who may represent all living creatures. It also includes the community of the redeemed, represented by twenty-four elders wearing garments of holiness and crowns of victory. The Elders may also represent the twelve patriarchs of the Old Testament era and the twelve apostles of the New Testament period (Revelation 21:12,14).

But there is more. Without explanation, both God the Father and the Lamb of God inhabit the heavenly throne. The Lamb represents none other than Jesus Christ, the triumphant Redeemer who, with the Father, governs the entire universe (Ephesians 1:22-23). His seven horns and seven eyes symbolize his complete authority, omnipotence, and omnipresence. The congregation, including countless angels, worships the Lamb, singing "Worthy is the Lamb, who was slain, to receive power and wealth and wisdom and strength and honor and glory and praise" (Revelation 5:12). That worship serves as a prelude to the "praise and honor and glory and power" rendered by every creature in heaven and on earth and under the earth and on the sea. Such is the future of the redeemed.

Until that time we, the Militant Church, the imperfect church, the adulterous bride of Christ, worship the Lord with our frail voices, divided attentions, limited understandings, and nagging sins. We do the best we can, trusting that God the Holy Spirit will compensate for our weaknesses and, thereby, enable us to worship in spirit and in truth. Occasionally our worship seems heavenly and we leave the gathered community saying, "It's been good to be in the house of the Lord." Like Jacob who wrestled with God, we come away from "church" convinced that we experienced a genuine encounter with the Lord.

But that is not always the case. Sometimes we leave worship muttering words like "I got nothing out of that." It is then we remind ourselves that subjective feelings fail to accurately measure the effectiveness of a liturgy. It is then we draw upon our faith in God who works mysteriously and, sometimes, imperceptibly. It is then that we rest in God's promise that His Word accomplishes its objective, whether we feel it or not. As Isaiah recorded,

> As the rain and the snow come down from heaven, and do not return to it without watering the earth and making it bud and flourish, so that it

yields seed for the sower and bread for the eater, so is my word that goes out from my mouth: It will not return to me empty, but will accomplish what I desire and achieve the purpose for which I sent it (55:10-11).

Our faith in God's sovereignty over worship does not take us off the hook. God still expects us to work at our worship. He calls us to continuously review and evaluate our liturgies, to reflect on how best to worship the Lord in this life. So, we will study and evaluate, pray and plan. We will seek to minimize the influence of our weaknesses and maximize the grandeur of the One we worship. We will, as someone once said, "do our best and let God do the rest."

One day we will not have to work at our worship. As foretold in Revelation 21, we will dwell in the new heaven and the new earth. We will worship in the New Jerusalem. John's vivid and detailed description of that Holy City has led some to miss a very important truth: the New Jerusalem is not a place, but a people. It is not the final home of the redeemed; it is the redeemed. The New Jerusalem is a symbol of the bride, the church. It is a real and precious community of individuals who have direct and immediate fellowship with God. Through his vision, John assures us that in heaven, we will be His people, and God himself will be with us and be our God (21:3).

In the time between now and our eternal worship, may the Lord grant us humility to recognize that, even following our best efforts, our liturgical practices will always reflect our shortcomings and sins. May the Lord grant us wisdom to discern them through the knowledge of His good and perfect will. May He then grant us the courage of the Reformers to identify and forsake our idols until that day we behold Him. Then we will not have to work so hard at our worship. We will, as glorified saints, join all of the redeemed in perpetual praise to our Triune God.

Appendix
Developing the Liturgy
One Congregation's Journey

Introduction

During its last decade, the Palos Heights Christian Reformed Church has wrestled long and hard with a variety of innovations, while seeking to remain faithful to the biblical principles that, to one degree or another, shape the corporate response of God's people to His mercy and grace. If I break that process into neat pieces I betray the give and take, the providential interruptions, the backward steps, the mistakes, the confusion, the long and winding road, the overlapping, and more. But, looking back, I see basic steps through which God led us by His Word and Spirit.

I share our journey with you for, as one preacher said, "Your message may electrify and edify, but it better specify." So, here are the ingredients that went into the mixing bowl that, by God's grace and in His time, produced our liturgy.

The Skeleton For Worship

One of the earliest steps in the development of corporate liturgy is the determination of the skeleton or order for worship. Minimally, every liturgy includes three parts: the gathering, worship, and the dismissal. For some, that's enough. They choose not to dissect their unique combination of liturgical actions any further. From that position, they determine the liturgical actions essential to the second movement called "worship." Michael Horton, among many others, opts for this approach. Following his conviction that worship is a covenant renewal ceremony, he proposes that the order of worship follow that of the Old Testament covenant renewal services.[1] Building on the "types and shadows of the Old Testament," Horton opts to list the following as essential liturgical actions, rather than speak of movements:

The Invocation
God's Greeting
The Law
Confession and Absolution
The Pastoral Prayer
The Preached Word
The Ministry of the Lord's Supper
Thanksgiving and Offerings
The Benediction[2]

There is some merit to Horton's approach. When Christians divide the worship of God's people into labeled sections, they distort reality. Labels, while convenient, seldom represent the whole truth. Worship, like love, can not be sliced into neat, discernable pieces. When we hear the Law, we hear God's Word. When we praise the Lord, we grow in the grace and knowledge of the Lord. When we witness our faith in Christ, we serve our neighbor. When we offer our gifts or confess our sins, we praise the Lord.

While recognizing their limitations, however, most Christian traditions have found that labels increase the formative power of the liturgy in, at least, three ways. First, labels simplify that which might appear complex.

---

[1] Michael Horton, *A Better Way: Rediscovering the Drama of Christ-Centered Worship*, 24.
[2] Michael Horton, *A Better* Way, 147-160.

Appendix

By labeling the movements, worshipers receive assistance in connecting the purposes of the individual parts within the whole. This, in turn, minimizes the potential for participation without understanding or, what some call, "going through the motions." Second, labels cultivate an understanding about the dramatic flow and purpose of the liturgy. By labeling the movements, we accent important theological truths about corporate worship including the teaching that the liturgy is not an end in itself. Third, labels help worship leaders plan the liturgy so that the end result is not a smorgasbord of liturgical elements without direction.

Robert Webber, a leader in the study of Christian worship, believes that, for centuries, the liturgy has included four movements which, together, retell the "biblical story of God's initiating a relationship with fallen humanity.[3] They are:

Assembling the People
Listening and Responding to God's Word
Remembering and Giving Thanks
Going Forth to Love and Serve the Lord

Many Reformed Christians believe that the fundamental purpose for worship is to hear the Word of the Lord.[4] Their liturgies, then, include three basic movements, often labeled as Guilt, Grace and Gratitude, corresponding to the three movements of the Heidelberg Catechism. The movements are:

The Approach to God
The Word of God
The Response to the Word

The Church of Christ, and others like them, discover their order for worship in Acts 2:42 where they find the First Church of Jerusalem devoting itself "to the apostles' teaching and to the fellowship, to the breaking of bread and to prayer." Once gathered, these Christians: fellowship by uniting their voices in song, receive an apostolic "lesson" or teaching from the preacher, receive the sacrament of the Lord's Supper, and pray.

---

[3] Robert Webber, *Worship Old & New*, 149.
[4] See Edmund Clowney, "The Biblical Theology of the Church," *The Church in the Bible and the World* (Grand Rapids, MI: Baker Book House, 1993), 16-24.

Principled Worship

Many contemporary evangelical congregations follow a simple pattern, one espoused centuries ago by the Reformers, of praise, prayer and proclamation. Once gathered, the saints praise the Lord with their songs and gifts. The singing can go anywhere from ten minutes to nearly an hour. Then, they offer their prayers for one another and the world; though the prayer of confession is often omitted. Finally, they receive God's Word through the reading of Scripture, a sermon and, occasionally, through the Lord's Supper.

My congregation, the Palos Heights Christian Reformed Church has adopted a five-act order for worship, labeled in the following manner:

God Calls Us To Worship
We Praise The Lord
God Offers His Grace
We Witness Our Faith
God Sends Us Out To Serve

That five-movement outline flows directly from our life as the people of God. We have covenanted through baptism and profession of faith "to love as we have been loved." In fulfillment of that mission, we strive to reach five goals. Our liturgy includes five movements that correspond to those five goals. By God's grace we hope to:
1. Embrace and enjoy the communion of the Holy Spirit (fellowship),
2. Praise the Lord (worship),
3. Grow in the grace of the Lord (discipleship),
4. Testify to God's grace as the salt and light of the world (witness), and
5. Serve both God and neighbor (service).

The relationship between the liturgy and our corporate life is not accidental. It flows from the conviction that the liturgy of a particular congregation remembers and expresses its life in the Lord. Hence, this liturgy is descriptive rather than prescriptive. In this vein, some might refer to it as a "characterizing activity" that distinguishes us from other local congregations. We might also refer to it as "paradigmatic" in that

Appendix

it offers a paradigm, or framework, in which to understand our life and ministry as a corporate body.[5]

The Liturgical Actions

At the same time, or shortly after, a congregation determines its order for worship, she must determine her list of essential liturgical actions. The list of possibilities has remained pretty standard over the years, but the options are endless in that nearly every liturgical action may be offered in several modes:
  Spoken or sung by one, some or all,
  Extemporaneously (free) or as a formed reading, and
  While seated, standing or kneeling.

Here is a master list of liturgical actions, categorized according to the five movement liturgy of the Palos Heights Christian Reformed Church.

God Calls Us Together For Worship
  Preparation – Silent Or Otherwise
  Washing Of Feet
  Welcome
  Acknowledgement Of Guests
  Reception Of New Members
  Mutual Greeting Or Passing The Peace
  Announcements
  Call To Worship
  Prayer For Illumination Or Invocation
  The Lord's Prayer

We Praise The Lord
  Congregational Singing Of Psalms
  Congregational Singing Of Hymns

---

[5] See Craig R. Dyksra, *Vision and Character* (New York: Paulist Press, 1981).

Principled Worship

Congregational Singing Of Spiritual Songs
Choir Anthem Or Vocal Solo
Unison Or Responsive Readings Of Praise
Offering
Creedal Profession Of Faith
Prayer Of Confession

God Offers His Grace

Service Of Reconciliation
    Call To Worship
    Prayer Of Confession
    Words Of Assurance
Scripture Lessons
Sermon
Children's Sermon
Sharing Of Concerns Or Announcements
Congregational Prayer
The Lord's Prayer
The Sacrament Of Baptism
The Sacrament Of The Lord's Supper
Prayers For Healing Or The Anointing Of The Sick
Invitation To Faith
Ordination Service

We Witness Our Faith

Tithes And Offerings
Musical Offertory
Testimony
Confirmation Or Profession Of Faith
Creedal Profession
Congregational Songs Of Thanks
Sacrament Of Baptism

God Sends Us Out To Serve

Summary Of God's Will
Offerings
Mission Presentation

Appendix

Commissioning Service
Benediction
Parting Song
Passing Of The Peace
Prayer

Once a worship planning team has determined its list of essential liturgical actions, as well as their mode of operation, they may be placed within the predetermined order of worship. It is here that the liturgy takes shape, reflecting its unique context among a unique people. Here is how the process developed with my congregation. Notice, I have two columns. The one on the left is the ideal liturgy developed in the "ivory tower." The congregation employed it for several months. The liturgy on the right is that which evolved a few months later after receiving valid concerns from loving and sincere saints.

God Calls Us Together For Worship

Welcome	Welcome
Mutual Greeting	Mutual Greeting
Announcements	Call to Worship
Call To Worship	Opening Hymn
Prayer For Illumination	Invocation
The Lord's Prayer (unison)	The Lord's Prayer (unison)

We Praise The Lord

Congregational Singing	Congregational Singing
Unison Readings	Prayer of Confession (unison)
Choir Anthem	Choir Anthem/Ministry of Music
	Announcements
	Congregational Prayer
	Tithes and Offerings

God Offers His Grace

Prayer of Confession	Prayer for Illumination
Scripture Lesson	Scripture Lesson
Sermon	Sermon
Congregational Prayer	Prayer - Blessing Upon the Word
The Sacraments	The Sacraments

Principled Worship

We Witness Our Faith

Tithes and Offerings	Profession of Faith
Musical Offertory	Congregational Song
Profession of Faith	
Congregational Song	

God Sends Us Out To Serve

Summary of God's Will	Summary of God's Will
Benediction	Benediction
Parting Song	Parting Song

Principle Driven Worship

The process of determining the movements of worship and the liturgical actions within each one cannot be separated from the biblical roots that shape the weekly gathering of God's people. Rather than review each principle in this volume and suggest its appropriate weight in your congregation's liturgy, I will highlight those biblical principles that significantly influenced the liturgy of the Palos Heights Christian Reformed Church.

First, as an evangelical congregation in the Reformed tradition, our liturgy accents the supremacy of the sermon. We believe that the center piece of the liturgy is the Word of God. We gather each week expecting to receive a word from the Lord. For us, the Proclaimed Word is the main course, but it is not the only ministry of the Word. We hope to receive God's Word in the reading of the Scriptures, through the sacraments, and even through the ministry of music.

Second, as a congregation in the Reformed tradition, we believe confession of sin to be an essential form of praise. Through this prayer we humble ourselves before the Lord, acknowledging His righteousness and our sinfulness, seeking His grace for the forgiveness of sins. We hope to receive assurance that, in spite of our waywardness, God will never leave or forsake us. As for the form of our confession, we prefer a mode that involves as many people as possible. So, we may sing our confession or offer it in unison or as a responsive reading, often employing formed prayers with historic roots, thereby accenting our membership in the one, holy, catholic and apostolic church.

Appendix

Third, as a Reformed congregation that believes God calls each believer to service in the world, our liturgy sends each believer back home with God's blessing. This is the place where we have experienced the most change in our liturgical life. For decades, our congregation concluded worship with a song of praise, like the "Doxology," or with a prayer like "God be with us till we meet again." But, after reflecting on our biblical roots, we began looking for more of a send off, like the officer sending the troops out to battle or the coach sending the team to the court, or the college president sending his graduates out to work. So now, we often use Jesus' summary of the Law as a reminder that God has called us to love him by loving our neighbor, which is the "third use" of the Law, a uniquely Reformed doctrine. We also join our voices in a "sending" song that clearly articulates God's desire that we return to our vocations to serve Him.

Fourth, as the body of Christ we believe that God calls us to offer hospitality to all who visit us, believing that the stranger or guest may be Christ himself. Through both announcements and prayers, we accent the potential interaction between Christ the Church and Christ the Stranger. Our liturgy accents the presence of guests in two ways. First, we welcome them in the name of Jesus Christ, offering them hope to receive the grace of the Lord through their time with us. Second, we pray for them. Our pastoral prayer almost always includes a petition that our guests hear Christ's Word in the liturgy and experience Christ's touch through His people.

Fifth, as a Reformed congregation that affirms the priesthood of all believers, we believe that liturgical leadership should be gift-based. In other words, those who lead worship should be gifted by the Holy Spirit for such service. They may or may not be ordained. Our non-ordained Minister of Music, for example, leads worship with me. Each week non-ordained, but gifted, communicators offer the "Prayer for Illumination" and scripture reading. When I am absent, gifted Elders offer the "Congregational Prayer."

Sixth, as a congregation suspicious of fads and sensitive to sacred space, we have taken a minimalist approach to technology believing that less is better. There are several reasons for this approach. First, with limited financial resources, we have chosen to invest money in pastors and programs, rather than in technology and professionals to run it. Second, the installation of some of the more popular forms of technology, like projectors and screens, would negatively impact the aesthetics of our worship space. They just don't fit. Third, worship planning not only becomes more challenging when adding more technology, it also becomes less flexible. We tend to go "with the flow." I have been known, for example, to change my sermon significantly from one service to the next, or to add a song from the hymn book. Scripted services, dialed into power point, strips away any opportunity for improvisation prompted by the Holy Spirit.

Seventh, as a Reformed congregation with a heritage of minimizing the third person of the Trinity, we have chosen to accent the role of the Holy Spirit, hopefully without reducing the primacy of Christ. We highlight the Holy Spirit in our prayers by acknowledging that, without the Spirit, we are wasting our time, and by claiming God's promise to do more than we could ever ask or imagine. The first movement of the liturgy includes a prayer by which we confess our limitations and invoke the Spirit's blessing upon our worship. The third movement of the liturgy includes a prayer for illumination whereby we acknowledge the blinders on our eyes and claim the promise of Jesus that the Spirit will guide us into all truth.

Eighth, as a congregation seeking to be faithful to scripture within a narcissistic culture, we believe that worship is corporate. I like to say, "worship is not about me, it is about us." We are not spectators, but performers. The conviction that worship is corporate radically influences how we gather for worship and how we receive our guests. It shapes the ordering of our liturgical actions and helps us select the songs we sing. It influences the modes by which we worship the Lord and the process by which we select volunteers to support worship. We want each congregant to actively participate in as much of the liturgy as possible.

Each of those principles has significantly influenced the liturgy that emerged among us over a four year period. But, to one degree or another, so has each principle identified in this volume. They represent the biblical roots of our liturgical life.

Lessons Learned

We learned several lessons through our process of liturgical renewal. First, we discovered that practicalities have a way of shaping the liturgy. Our congregation, for example, has two identical morning worship services.

Appendix

The first service begins at 9 AM, and the second at 10:30 AM. That schedule greatly impacts the technicians, worship leaders, and musicians, some of whom arrive as early as 8 AM. Out of sensitivity to them, we try to have "special" music completed before the sermon so that the majority of musicians need but attend one and a half services. For that same reason we moved up the offering. In our setting, the Deacons receive the financial offerings. By placing the offering at the end of the service, we were never quite sure if we would have enough Deacons to receive it. So, we moved it up in the liturgy and frame it as an act of praise to the Lord, the giver of every good and perfect gift.

Second, we discovered that a congregation can handle **planned** change if assured that it comes through proper protocol and when prepared for such change. Worship is the most intimate experience of the Christian's corporate life. It is loaded with emotion. Therefore, it cannot be addressed haphazardly, without proper authority, without discretion, and without communication. The major parts of the liturgy cannot change week to week based on the whims of one person.

I remember my first Christmas Day service in Palos Heights. When planning the liturgy, a staff member suggested we close the service with the Dutch song "Glory to God." That seemed like a good suggestion for a congregation with Dutch roots. Christmas Day came and I led my first Christmas service with my new congregation. After the service, I went to the back of the center aisle to receive some love. To my surprise, I didn't get much. I discovered then that, up to that moment in time, the Palos Heights Christian Reformed Church had concluded every Christmas Day service with Handel's "Hallelujah Chorus," sung by the choir and by anyone else who would like to join the choir. Many gathered that morning expecting to sing with their children, parents, and grandchildren. Needless to say, we have sung the "Hallelujah Chorus" every Christmas Day since.

The third lesson learned is somewhat related to the second. We discovered that congregants can handle weekly change within the movements of the liturgy, but resist weekly change to the order of the movements themselves. If you think that unusual, ask yourself what happens when your favorite television newscast changes its format from news, weather and sports to something else. Or how would you respond if, while dining at a nice restaurant, your salad came after the main course? Christians, like all people, are creatures of habit. We prefer the familiar over the unknown. So when we gather for worship, we like to know the lay of the land. The benefit of such knowledge is that it frees us from concerns about structure so that we can focus our attention on worship. The greater the familiarity one has with the liturgy, the greater the potential for wholehearted worship.

Fourth, we learned the liturgy of a congregation is so profoundly shaped by the nature of the gathered community that every liturgy becomes a unique expression of love. Our gathered community is multi-generational, including children. It also includes many mentally-impaired adults. When planning the liturgy, we wanted as many people as possible involved in worship. I begin each service with a responsive reading from Psalm 113, calling each participant to praise the Lord with his or her "Hallelujah." We often couple the "Lord's Prayer" with our opening prayer of invocation, asking the congregation to offer those precious words in unison. Over time, the little children learn this prayer and join their voices with all of God's people, and the mentally impaired adults speak it louder than all the rest. The prayers of all God's people in unison create a delightful sound.

Conclusion

So, there it is. One congregation, with its unique culture and context, led by one pastor, with his unique baggage, coming together in a specific time and place, seeking to worship the Lord "on the terms he proposes and in the manner that he makes possible."[6] This volume reflects the heart and soul of that process. It reveals the liturgy that emerged from biblical roots in a twenty-first century congregation.

But this much I am sure of: our work is not done. Prompted by the Holy Spirit, we will come under conviction of sin. We will, then, lament our idolatrous ways, our fake sacrifices, our split personalities, our failure to worship in Spirit and in truth. Prompted by the desire to love the Lord and our neighbor, we will always work at our worship. We will sift our liturgies through God's Word. We will always be reforming.

---

[6] David Peterson, *Engaging With God: A Biblical Theology of Worship* (Downers Grove, IL: InterVarsity Press, 1992), 283.

Appendix

That's one reason why heaven appeals to me. The eternal Sabbath, when we see the Lord face to face, when we gather with the one, holy, catholic, apostolic Church, offers the opportunity to worship without working so hard at it. We will simply join those who have been at it for an eternity.

Until that day, may the Lord, by His grace, keep us faithful. And when we walk away from the Lord and fall, may He compensate for our shortcomings so that His glory shines undiminished by our sins.

Selective Bibliograpy On Worship

Allen, Horace T., "Calendar and Lectionary in Reformed Perspective and History," in *Christian Worship in Reformed Churches Past and Present*, edited by Lukas Vischer (Grand Rapids, MI: Eerdmans Publishing Co., 2003), 397.

Anderson, E. Byron and Morrill, Bruce T., editors. *Liturgy and the Moral Self*, Collegeville: MN, The Liturgical Press, 1998.

Anderson, E. Byron. "O for a heart to praise my God': Hymning the Self Before God" in *Liturgy and the Moral Self*, edited by E Byron Anderson and Bruce T. Morrill. Collegeville: MN, The Liturgical Press, 1998.

Authentic Worship in a Changing Culture. Grand Rapids, MI: CRC Publications, 1997.

Barth, Karl. *Church Dogmatics: The Doctrine of Reconciliation*, translated by G.W. Bromiley (London: T&T Clark, 1961).

Basden, Paul, editor. *Exploring the Worship Spectrum: Six Views* (Grand Rapids, MI: Zondervan Publishing Co., 2004.

Bilezikian, Gilbert. *Community 101: Reclaiming the Local Church as Community of Oneness*. Grand Rapids, MI: Zondervan Publishing Co., 1997.

Bloesch, Donald. *The Church: Sacraments, Worship, Ministry, Mission*. Downers Grove, IL: InterVarsity Press, 2002.

___. *The Holy Spirit: Works and Gifts*. Downers Grove, IL: InterVarsity Press, 2000.

Borgmann, Albert. *Power Failure: Christianity in the Culture of Technology*. Grand Rapids, MI: Brazos Books, 2003.

Brink, Emily R. and Witvliet, Emily R. "Music in Reformed Churches Worldwide," in *Christian Worship in Reformed Churches Past and Present*, edited by Lukas Vischer. Grand Rapids, MI: Eerdmans Publishing Co., 2003.

Bibliography

Brown, Frank Burch Brown. *Good Taste, Bad Taste, and Christian Taste: Aesthetics in the Religious Life*. New York: Oxford University Press, 2000.

Bruggink, Donald J. and Droppers, Carl H. *Christ and Architecture: Building Presbyterian/Reformed Churches* (Grand Rapids, MI: Eerdmans Publishing Company, 1965).

Burghardt, Walter J. "Worship and Justice Reunited," in *Liturgy and Justice: To Worship God in Spirit and Truth*, edited by Anne Y. Koester. Collegeville, MN: The Liturgical Press, 2002.

Calvin, John. *The Institutes of Christian Religion.*

____. *Necessity of Reforming the Church*. Dallas, TX: Protestant Heritage Series, 1995.

Carson, D.A. and Kelly, Timothy, Ashton, Mark, and Hughes, R. Kent. *Worship by the Book*. Grand Rapids, MI: Zondervan, 2002.

Clapp, Rodney. *A Peculiar People: The Church as culture in a post-Christian society*. Downers Grove, IL: InterVarsity Press, 1966.

Clark, D. Marion. "Baptism: Joyful Sign of the Gospel," in *Give Praise to God: A Vision For Reforming Worship*, edited by Philip Graham Ryken, Derek W.H. Thomas, and J. Ligon Duncan III. Phillipsburg, PA: P&R Publishing, Inc, 2003.

Clowney, Edmund. *The Church*. Downers Grove, IL: InterVarsity Press, 1995.

____. *The Church in the Bible and the World* (Grand Rapids, MI: Baker Book House, 1993).

Cooke, Bernard. *Ministry to Word and Sacraments: History and Theology*. Philadelphia: Fortress Press, 1976.

Dawn, Marva. *The Hilarity of Community; Romans 12 and How to Be the Church*. Grand Rapids, MI: Eerdmans Publishing Co., 1992.

____. *How Shall We Worship? Biblical Guidelines for the Worship Wars* (Wheaton, IL: Tyndale Publishers, 2003).

____. *Reaching Out Without Dumbing Down: A Theology of Worship for the Turn-Of-The-Century Culture*. Grand Rapids, MI: Eerdmans Publishing, Co., 1995.

____. *A Royal Waste of Time: The Splendor of Worshiping God and Being the Church for the World*. Grand Rapids, MI: Eerdmans Publishing, Co., 1999.

____. *Unfettered Hope: A Call to Faithful Living in an Affluent Society* (Louisville, KY: Westminster John Knox Press, 2003).

de Gruchy, John W. "Holy Beauty: A Reformed Perspective on Aesthetics within a World of Ugly Injustice," in *Reformed Theology for the Third Christian Millennium*, edited by B.A. Gerrish. Westminster John Knox Press, 2003.

Dyrness, William A. *Visual Faith: Art, Theology, and Worship in Dialogue*. Grand Rapids, MI: Baker Book House, 2001.

Edwards, Jonathan. "Religious Affections," in *The Works of Jonathan Edwards, Volume 2,* edited by John E. Smith (New Haven, CT: Yale University Press, 1959).

Finney, Charles. *Lectures on Revivals of Religion.* William G. McLoughlin, ed. Cambridge, Massachusetts: Harvard University, Belknap Press, 1960.

Frankforter, A. Daniel. *Stones for Bread: A Critique of Contemporary Worship* (Louisville, KY: Westminster John Knox Press, 2001).

Fremont, Paul. *Belonging and Not Belonging: The Creative Margins* (January 2, 2003).

Hageman, Howard. *Pulpit and Table.* Richmond, Virginia: John Knox Press, 1962.

Hamstra, Sam, Jr. "Altar Calls and Effectual Calls." *Modern Reformation* (July/August 1998), 19-22.

____, editor. *The Reformed Pastor: Lectures on Pastoral Theology by John Williamson Nevin* (Eugene, Oregon: Wiph & Stock Publishers, 2006).

Hart, D.G. *Recovering Mother Kirk: The Case for Liturgy in the Reformed Tradition* (Grand Rapids, MI: Bake Book House, 2003).

Hart, D.G. and Muether, John R. *With Reverence and Awe: Returning to the Basics of Reformed Worship.* Phillipsburg, NJ: P&R Publishing, 2002.

Hauerwas, Stanley. "Worship, Evangelism, Ethics: On Eliminating the 'And'," in *Liturgy and the Moral Self,* edited by E. Byron Anderson and Bruce T. Morrill. Collegeville: MN, The Liturgical Press, 1998.

Horton, Michael. *A Better Way: Rediscovering the Drama of Christ-Centered Worship.* Grand Rapids, MI: Baker Book House, 2002.

Keifert, Patrick. *Welcoming the Stranger: A Public Theology of Worship and Evangelism* (Minneapolis: MN: Fortress Press, 1992).

Kimball, Dan. *Emerging Worship: Creating Worship Gatherings for New Generations.* (Grand Rapids, MI: Zondervan Publishing, Co., 2004).

Küng, Hans. *The Church.* Garden City, NY: Image Books, 1976.

Kuiper, R.B. *The Glorious Body of Christ.* Grand Rapids, MI: Eerdmans Publishing Co.

Kuyper, Abraham. *The Work of the Holy Spirit,* translated by Henri De Vries. Grand Rapids, MI: Eerdmans Publishing Co., 1979.

Long, Thomas G. *Beyond the Worship Wars: Building Vital and Faithful Worship.* The Alban Institute, 2001.

Macleod, Donald. "Calvin into Hipplytus," in *To Glorify God: Essays on Modern Reformed Liturgy,* edited by Bryan D. Spinks and Iain R. Torrance. Grand Rapids, MI: Eerdmans Publishing Co, 1999.

Marini, Stephen A. *Sacred Song in America: Religion, Music, Public Culture.* Champaign, IL: University of Illinois, 2003.

Bibliography

Maxwell, Jack M. *Worship and Reformed Theology: The Liturgical Lessons of Mercersburg.* Pittsburgh: The Pickwick Press, 1976.

McKee, Elsie Anne. "Reformed Worship in the Sixteenth Century," in *Christian Worship in Reformed Churches Past and Present,* edited by Lukas Vischer. Grand Rapids, MI: Eerdmans Publishing Co, 2003.

Moltmann, Jürgen. *The Source of Life: The Holy Spirit and the Theology of Life.* Translated by Margaret Kohl from the German, *Die Quelle des Lebens: Der Heilige Geist und die Theologie des Lebens.* Minneapolis, MN: Augsburg Fortress Press, 1997.

Morgenthaler, Sally. *Worship Evangelism: Inviting Unbelievers into the Presence of God* (Grand Rapids, MI: Zondervan Publishing Co., 1995).

Nevin, John W. *The Anxious Bench.* 2nd ed. Chambersburg, PA: Publication Office of the German Reformed Church, 1844.

___. "Doctrine of the Reformed Church on the Lord's Supper." The Mercersburg Review 2 (1850): 421-548.

___. *The Mystical Presence, a Vindication of the Reformed or Calvinistic Doctrine of the Holy Eucharist.* Philadelphia, 1846.

___. "A Vindication of the Revised Liturgy." In *Catholic and Reformed: Selected Theological Writings of John Williamson Nevin,* edited by Charles Yrigoyen Jr. and George H. Bricker (Pittsburgh, PA: The Pickwick Press, 1978).

Newbigin, Leslie. *The Gospel in a Pluralistic Society.* Grand Rapids, MI: Eerdmans Publishing Co, 1989.

___. *The Household of God.* New York: Friendship Press, 1953.

Nouwen, Henri. *Reaching Out.* New York: Doubleday & Company, Inc., 1975.

Old, Hughes Oliphant. *Worship Reformed according to Scripture.* Louisville, KY: Westminster John Knox Press, 2002.

David Peterson. *Engaging With God: A Biblical Theology of Worship* (Downers Grove, IL: InterVarsity Press, 1992).

Plantinga, Jr., Cornelius, and Rozeboom, Sue A. *Discerning the Spirits: A Guide to Thinking About Christian Worship Today.* Grand Rapids, MI: Eerdmans Publishing Co. 2003.

Pohl, Christine. *Making Room: Recovering Hospitality as a Christian Tradition* (Grand Rapids, MI: Eerdmans Publishing Co, 1999).

Postman, Neil. *Technopoly: The Surrender of Culture to Technology.* New York: Vantage Books, 1992.

Rice, Howard L. and James C. Huffstutler. *Reformed Worship.* Louisville, KY: Geneva Press, 2001.

Ryken, Philip Graham, and Derek W.H. Thomas, J. Ligon Duncan III, eds. *Give Praise to God: A Vision for Reforming Worship.* Phillipsburg, NJ: P&R Publishing, 2003.

Saliers, Don. "Liturgy and Ethics: Some New Beginnings," in *Liturgy and the Moral Self*, edited by E Byron Anderson and Bruce T. Morrill. Collegeville: MN, The Liturgical Press, 1998.

Scarry, Elaine. *On Beauty and Being Just*. Princeton: Princeton University Press, 1999.

Schmemann, Alexander. *For the Life of the World: Sacraments and Orthodoxy*. Crestwood, NY: St Vladimir's Seminary Press, 2002.

Schultze, Quentin. *High-Tech Worship? Using Presentational Technologies Wisely*. (Grand Rapids, MI: Baker Book House, 2004).

Spinks, Bryan D. and Iain R. Torrance, eds. *To Glorify God: Essays on Modern Reformed Liturgy*. Grand Rapids, MI: Eerdmans Publishing Co, 1999.

Vander Zee, Leonard. *Christ, Baptism and the Lord's Supper: Recovering the Sacraments for Evangelical Worship*. Downers Grove, IL: InterVarsity Press, 2004.

Van Dyk, Leanne, editor. *A More Profound Alleluia: Theology And Worship In Harmony*. Grand Rapids, MI: Baker Book House, 2005.

Vann, Jane. *Gathered Before God: Worship-Centered Church Renewal*. Louisville, KY: John Knox Press, 2004.

Vischer, Lukas, editor. *Christian Worship in Reformed Churches Past and Present*. Grand Rapids, MI: Eerdmans Publishing Co, 2003.

Webber, Robert. *Evangelicals on the Canterbury Trail: Why Evangelicals Are Attracted to the Liturgical Church*. Waco, TX: Word Publishing, 1985.

___. *Worship is a Verb: Eight Principles for Transforming Worship*. Peabody, MA: Hendrickson Publishers, 1992.

White, James F. "How Do We Know It Is Us?," in *Liturgy and The Moral Self*, edited by E. Byron Anderson and Bruce T. Morrill. Collegeville, MN: The Liturgical Press, 1998.

Witvliet, John D. "A Discerning Spirit: Making Good Choices in an Era of Liturgical Change." *Books and Culture* (September/October 2003), 22-26.

___. *Worship Seeking Understanding: Windows Into Christian Practice*. Grand Rapids, MI: Baker Book House, 2003.

Wood, David, "Prime Time: Albert Borgmann on Taming Technology," *The Christian Century* 120 (August 23, 2003).

Worship Sourcebook. Grand Rapids, MI: CRC Publications, 2004.

Wright, N.T. *For All God's Worth: True Worship and the Calling of the Church*. Grand Rapids, MI: Eerdmans, Publishing, Co., 1997.

www.ingramcontent.com/pod-product-compliance
Lightning Source LLC
Chambersburg PA
CBHW072155160426
43197CB00012B/2387